GROWTH
IN THE
HOLY SPIRIT

GROWTH
IN THE
HOLY SPIRIT

GERARD HUYGHE
Bishop of Arras

Translated by
Isabel and Florence McHugh

copy 2

NP

THE NEWMAN PRESS
WESTMINSTER, MARYLAND
1966

Originally published 1964 by Les Editions du Cerf, Paris,
under the title *Conduits par l'Esprit*.

First published this edition 1966
© translation 1966 Geoffrey Chapman Ltd.

Library of Congress Catalog Card Number: 66-17358.

Nihil Obstat R. D. Dermitius Fogarty, D.D., L.C.L., censor deputatus.
Imprimatur H. Gibney, Vicarius Generalis.
Datum Southwarci die 15a Septembris 1965.

Set in 12 on 14 pt. Bembo.

Made and printed in Great Britain

Contents

Foreword

THESE pages owe everything to the priests, religious, and lay apostles with whom I have spoken for so many years in the course of my duties as spiritual director, in encouraging lay groups, and in giving retreats. Together we have learned to interpret the events of our lives in the light of holy scripture in order to discover there the guiding thread of God's plan for us: the continual teaching activity of the Holy Spirit in our souls.

All these discoveries continued to take shape and merge in my subconscious until the day when circumstances led me to put them down in writing.

In August 1963 bad weather during the holiday which followed my annual retreat left me a great deal of time for reading and writing. By the end of this enforced solitude the greater part of this book was finished.

Its plan is simple. Within each of its five parts the ideas are grouped in the same way, but each succeeding part reviews the preceding ones in a new light. We trust that having considered the Holy Spirit's education of the faith of Abraham, of Mary, and finally of the apostles, the reader will be ready to recognize himself in the Christian of the twentieth century. For our faith grows constantly during the whole course of our lives, under the guidance of the Holy Spirit, by ways which follow the path traced for us in holy scripture.

Introduction

I. CHRISTIANITY, STATIC OR GROWING?

ALL too many baptized persons believe that Christianity is a stable body of doctrine which we hold permanently and need only cherish in order to keep a good conscience. Those whom we may call ritual practising Catholics belong to this category, in the sense that the practice of the Catholic religion, with its strict obligations, suits and reassures them.

The moralists, often confused with them, likewise belong here. For them religion is a moral code which they obey out of either habit or fear, but never out of love. Their morality is a minimum morality. They can distinguish very clearly between mortal and venial sin. They try to avoid the former, of course, but they reconcile themselves very easily to venial sin and for this reason the distinction between the two is very important for them. If they fall into mortal sin confession is an easy means of getting rid of it and beginning their narrow little lives again. Their Christianity runs in cycles; periodically they go through the same 'revolutions', but the cycles of today are exactly like those they went through twenty years ago. It is an 'endless round'. Their Christianity has something of the immobility of death. There is no

1. *Notre regard qui manque à la lumière*, p. 10.

dynamic principle in their faith. Everything has been given them in one go, and here again their 'good conscience', very like that of the Pharisees in our Lord's time, always bears witness in their favour. Their 'works' protect them from uneasiness.

Authentic Christianity, on the other hand, is a dynamic force, a growth. The whole of the Gospel teaches us this, not to mention the numerous parables or allegories which stress this aspect: the sower, the seed, the grain, the leaven in the dough. All the life which is in God is communicated to the soul on one single occasion—at baptism; it is implanted like a seed meant to grow. Its growth depends on the soil, in other words on the circumstances and environment of the person concerned. It may be stopped, deflected, suffocated, but it may also strike roots and fulfil the promise of the seed. It lasts throughout life, sometimes wilting, sometimes flourishing. It opens out into full bloom beyond the grave, when the baptized person participates, no longer by faith but with the fulness of the beatific vision, in the very life of God himself.

Once a Christian becomes aware that the divine life which has been given him is meant to grow, he enters on two stages of development.

The first, a more or less lengthy one, is a prolongation of the period preceding his spiritual awakening. Since his Christianity is to grow, he fixes an aim for this growth, which he calls by the very abstract name of sanctity; and he is convinced that he will attain to this state by his own powers. In this first stage he puts the accent on works carried out with a great deal of 'generosity', and gives a very secondary place to God's grace. But he must not remain there, for that is the path of Jansenist illusion or, more often, of discouragement and failure. Before his conversion this Christian did not know that the life he possessed was a growing thing at all. He probably did not even know that it was a life. He only saw his good works and his virtues, and his conscience had a death-like serenity. Now, under the action of grace, he discovers the dynamic character of the divine life and sets out courageously towards the goal he sees before him.

After this first stage, in which he tries to form new virtues to replace those that have collapsed and a new holiness to fill the void left by the liquidation of his complacent 'good conscience', failure, weakness, even sin make him intensely conscious of human frailty and his incapacity for good.

Now he enters on the second stage in which, quietly accepting the fact that he is a sinner but without resigning himself to it, he discovers with joy that he is a sinner saved. Never again will he have an easy conscience, and he will say with Isaiah: 'All our righteous deeds are like a polluted garment' (Is. lxiv, 6), or with St Paul: 'I am carnal, sold under sin. I do not understand my own actions. For I do not do what I want, but I do the very thing I hate . . . I can will what is right, but I cannot do it. For I do not do the good I want, but the evil I do not want is what I do . . . Wretched man that I am! Who will deliver me from this body of death? . . . It is the grace of God through Jesus Christ our Lord!' (Rom. vii, 14-25).

True, he will find peace, that peace which is the continual and unmerited gift of the mercy of God. The words 'personal merit' will be eliminated from his vocabulary. He will no longer speak of his virtues but only of his weakness, always making clear that he is saved from his own wretchedness by the mercy of God. He will no longer speak of 'his' personal holiness but of the holiness which is the exclusive attribute of the thrice-holy God and which is communicated to those who acknowledge their wretchedness.

The way is now open for a continuous growth. He will no longer try to take note of its signs in order to rejoice in them; instead he will abandon himself to God's generosity. For it is God himself, or rather the Holy Spirit, who animates this growth.

Let us turn to St Paul again: 'Any one who does not have the Spirit of Christ does not belong to him. But if Christ is in you . . . you will live. For all who are led by the Spirit of God are Sons of

God . . . but you have received the spirit of sonship. When we cry: "Abba! Father!" . . . the Spirit helps us in our weakness . . . the Spirit himself intercedes for us' (Rom. viii, 9-26).

One more point. We have been speaking of Christianity, the spiritual life, and the Christian life without making any distinction between them. They are common words with the same general meaning. But from now on we would prefer to speak of 'faith', which means the same thing but is the word most commonly used in the Bible. In the first part of this book we shall try to show how pregnant with meaning the word is. Suffice it to say here that faith is man's response to God's intervention. It is always God who takes the initiative. It is he who flings open the door of man's heart. It is he who calls and invites a response. And when man hears the call and decides to respond, he takes the road towards God under God's own direction; he begins to grow in faith and if he remains faithful, this growth never ceases.

II. A FAITH FOR TODAY

We have spoken of 'the school of faith'. The Christian in this school never comes to the end of his education under the direction of the Spirit of God. The curriculum is laid down in the Gospel: it is necessary for him, moreover, to keep on learning the lessons the whole length of his days, in the midst of events and human intercourse. And daily life is the place where he learns and the subject of instruction.

The only aim of the present work is to light up the path of the modern Christian in order that he may know to what the call of God commits him and the response that faith demands of him.

But if these pages are meant to be of present relevance, is it not rather strange to devote most of them to exploring the paths followed by Abraham, Mary and the apostles in the growth of their faith? Yet we are in fact contemporaries of these great believers, and their spiritual journey is reproduced in us. God undoubtedly adapts himself to temperaments and to actual situations, and the call he addresses to each individual is meant for that person alone. But the light which he reveals is the same for all, the spiritual hope he demands is always absolute, the fidelity he demands is always total, for God is always the same (Ps. ci, 27).

This is why, by trying to discover in the Bible how God educated Abraham, Mary and the apostles in the faith, we shall discover his methods of teaching and become capable of reading the map on which our own route is traced. We shall realize that, though generations pass and man changes, God remains the same. Further, in the last part of this book we shall try to see in the light of the past what the faith of the Christian of today—our own faith—should be, challenged as it is by an atmosphere of atheism and called on to provide an answer to the questions posed daily on all sides. The Christian feels the Pharisaical cloak of the 'good' conscience' slipping from his shoulders. People are looking for the face of Christ the Saviour and asking the baptized to reveal it to them. They will never be able to receive this revelation unless these baptized Christians attain a depth of faith that will enable them to recognize the features of Christ in all men, and the actions of Christ in people and events.

How will the salvation of Christ be brought to mankind today if the hope upon which Christians feed rises no higher than natural, human hope?

Mankind will only encounter and receive the love of God in the measure that Christians live it in their daily lives, loving their fellow-beings, all their fellow-beings, with a love not limited to words.

The faith of the Christian will not grow unless it is integrated with the whole of his own life and hence with the whole of the life of others. And it is in growing that it will bear witness.

I

What is a Growing Faith?

*'Creation is a work of God designed to
unite him with beings worthy of his love.'*
Henri Bergson

From Theological Faith to Biblical Faith

'O God, thou art my God, I seek thee,
my soul thirsts for thee:
my flesh faints for thee,
as in a dry and weary land where no
water is'

Ps. lxiii, 1.

I. THE CLASSICAL ACT OF FAITH

IN the modern view, faith is distinct from hope and charity. The three are theological virtues, each of which leads to God. Or, if you like, they are three different roads which lead to God, without any communication between them. True, theologians affirm that it is impossible to make a sincere act of faith without at the same time being full of hope and charity. But this is a theological proposition. What matters is how the propositions of the theologians are received and understood by the average Christian.

What is an authentic act of faith? We have all learned to say: 'My God, I firmly believe all the truths that you have revealed to us and that you teach us through your Church, because you can neither deceive nor be deceived.' There is a whole treatise of theology in this act of faith, but here we may note the following:

1. There is nothing in this text to indicate that there is any relation between faith, hope and charity. The proof of this is that, parallel with this act of faith, the catechism teaches us an act of hope and an act of charity.

2. This act of faith is an intellectual step, a declaration of adherence to truths affirmed *en bloc*. There is no reference in it

3

to a living God, no response to the word of God. The mind alone is engaged. The heart—in the Gospel sense of the word—is not gripped. It is quite possible to recite thousands of acts of faith without for one moment entering into prayer and dialogue with God.

3. Moreover, this intellectual adherence to dogmas affirmed once and for all dispenses the mind from taking stock of them and examining them in depth. Here again, it is quite possible to make thousands of acts of faith without knowing anything of what God has revealed, without having any desire to know it, or even having attained to a knowledge of Jesus Christ, who is the very truth incarnate.

4. Finally, this act of faith is like the dry grammar of the so-called living languages that is killed and cut up into abstract pieces for pupils to learn by heart.

Everything is said once and for all and no spiritual growth is possible, because none is assumed.

II. THE CALL OF GOD

In the Bible, every act of faith is preceded by a call of God, an initiative on the part of God. Thus, Abraham believed, but God had first intervened in his life and commanded him: 'Go from your country . . . And I shall make you a great nation . . .' (Gen. xii, 1-2). In the case of Mary: 'And blessed is she who believed . . .' (Luke i, 45); but before attaining to this faith she had received God's call through an angel. The call of God always comes first. The Bible shows us this very frequently. It shows us history, the history of certain human beings—Abraham and Mary, for instance—or of a certain race, the Jews, being suddenly transfixed by a radiant coming of God, by a message from him. The Bible is the crossroads where God and man meet, the place where the call of God rings out.

This call of God has many forms:

1. In one form it *tells us something about God:* 'I am who I am' (Ex. iii, 14); 'I am the living God', and 'Besides me there is no God' (Is. xlv); I am 'the God of Abraham, the God of Isaac, and the God of Jacob' (Ex. iii, 15); 'You are my witnesses . . . that you may know and believe me and understand that I am he' (Is. xliii, 10).

2. In another form it makes a *promise* which always has a dual fulfilment, temporal and eternal:

(a) A temporal fulfilment: 'And I will give to you, and to your descendants after you, the land of your sojournings, all the land of Canaan, for an everlasting possession; and I will be their God' (Gen. xvii, 8); 'And the Lord God will give to him the throne of his father David' (Luke i, 32).

(b) An eternal fulfilment: 'I will indeed bless you, and I will multiply your descendants as the stars of heaven and as the sand which is on the seashore . . . and by your descendants shall all the nations of the earth bless themselves' (Gen. xxii, 17-18); 'And of his kingdom there shall be no end' (Luke i, 33).

This promise is always accompanied by a declaration of God's omnipotence, which confirms and guarantees it. 'Is anything too hard for the Lord?' (Gen. xviii, 14), the three messengers of God ask Abraham and Sara.

'For with God nothing will be impossible', the Angel Gabriel says to Mary (Luke i, 37).

3. In yet another form God recalls each one of his previous interventions and affirms the continuity between these, declaring that *he is faithful.*

This is a term proper to God, as it were. He is the God faithful to his promises. He is the God of Abraham, of Isaac and of Jacob. He is the God of the patriarchs. And Jesus Christ himself is 'the faithful witness' (Rev. i, 5). Men change but God does not change. Men lie, God does not deceive. Men are weak and fickle, but God is a rock, the rock of ages upon which everything is built.

III. MAN GIVES HIS 'FAITH'

To these interventions on the part of God which mark the history of salvation, to this manifold call of God man is invited to respond with 'faith'. To this voice of God, which takes on such varied tones, man gives that all-embracing response, namely faith, which comprises everything we understand today under the words faith, hope and charity. This response is not given all at once. It begins one day in the form of a 'Yes'. At the call of God Abraham sets out on a journey, but the journey on which he starts is to last a whole lifetime, in the course of which he will reiterate his 'Yes' to calls which become progressively clearer and more exacting. And the devout consent which he will give to the will of God at the moment when he is about to sacrifice Isaac will have a different force from that which he had given at the moment of leaving his country and his people.

In the same way, Mary replies: 'I am the handmaid of the Lord' to the first call of the angel. But her 'Yes' at the moment of the death of her only son has a different force and a different depth from the reply she had made on the day of the annunciation.

For all those who hear a call from God—and that means all baptized persons—the first response is a seed which is to grow throughout their lives. The first act of faith is a grain of mustard seed, but it is already rich in all that the action of the Holy Spirit will draw from it as it grows. It comprises the three elements of the response to the three forms of the call of God with which we have just dealt.

1. Since this call is, in the first place, a revelation of the living God, our faith will be first and foremost *a discovery of the living God*, a certainty of his permanent intervention. During the whole of life the eyes of the soul will become more penetrating and more capable of recognizing this certitude of God's permanent intervention. Further, we who have known God through Jesus Christ will learn to distinguish the persons of the Father, of the Word

Incarnate, and of the Spirit of love, who will initiate us more and more deeply into their divine intimacy.

2. Since this call is a promise which rests on the omnipotence of God, our faith will be an ever stronger *hope*. This faith will grow in spite of our sins and failures, or rather through them, until a day comes when we agree to stake our lives on the word of God and to believe that to him nothing is impossible.

3. Finally, this call of God who is faithful demands the continual response of our own *faithfulness*. At the starting point of a route which we are to follow throughout our life it is easy to be faithful, for we are ignorant of what is to come and we do not know the obstacles which our sinfulness and selfishness will place in the way of our growth in faithfulness. We shall come to know failure, discouragement and perhaps even defeat itself. By this experience we shall perceive God's faithfulness in a new light and our own faithfulness will draw new strength from it.

The faith of the devout believer, which each of us should be, is a dynamic act, always increasing under the influence of the Spirit of God. As we have said, it has the elements for a threefold response to the three aspects of God's call: a permanent discovery of the richness of the living God, a progressive discovery of his omnipotence, and a marvellous discovery of his unchanging faithfulness.

These three elements are comprised in the unique act of faith which the Christian addresses to God on hearing the first call to conversion—an act of faith so full of meaning that the convert spends the rest of his life discovering its inherent power.

2.

Faith is a Discovery of the Living God

WHEN God calls, he sends a flash of light into the soul and causes an upheaval in the person's life. Before this call there was only darkness. Now all is light, but the convert must traverse the landscape that has just opened up before him.

This discovery of God is something so ineffable and overwhelming that we can express it only very imperfectly and inadequately. Nevertheless we shall try to describe some aspects of it.

1. It is, in the first place, a sudden *certainty* that God has intervened. The Bible shows us this frequently. Abraham knows that God has spoken to him: this is not just an opinion, a possibility, or even a probability; it is for him something obvious, and it engenders a calm certitude: it lights up his whole life, and inspires every step he takes. All the patriarchs have the same conviction, rooted in that of their fathers. The prophets say again and again: 'The Lord has spoken to me' and 'Thus says the Lord'. Mary lived all her humble life in the conviction that the Lord had done wonderful things in her. After the resurrection and ascension of Jesus, the apostles maintained the unshakable conviction that they had known the Son of God. All those who, at some moment of their lives, have experienced conversion in the sense of a personal call from God never doubt for an instant that they have once encountered him in this mysterious way.

2. This God they have encountered is the *'living God'*. These are the words that best express their experience. This is how God reveals himself. He is a 'someone', a living person, who speaks and acts. He wishes to be 'recognized' and 'understood'. We have already quoted the words he addressed to Israel: 'You are my

witnesses . . . that you may know and believe me and understand that I am he' (Is. xliii, 10).

This is equally clear in the Gospels. Jesus demands to be recognized. 'But who do you say that I am?' (Matt. xvi, 15), he asks his apostles. And Peter replies: 'You are the Christ, the Son of the living God' (Matt. xvi, 16). In the Old Testament the object of the light of faith is the living God who acts without ceasing. In the New Testament its object is Christ, the Son of God. Thus, when the Samaritan woman says to Jesus: 'I know that the Messiah is coming', he replies: 'I who speak to you am he' (John iv, 25-26). Jesus says to the man born blind: 'Do you believe in the Son of Man?' The man asks Jesus eagerly: 'And who is he, sir, that I may believe in him?' Jesus replies: 'You have seen him, and it is he who speaks to you.' The man thereupon falls on his knees before Jesus saying: 'Lord, I believe' (John ix, 35-38).

And since that time, in his Church, Christ has ceaselessly put the same question to those whose eyes he opens with a touch of his hand. 'Do you believe in me?' 'Who do you say that I am?' Unless faith is based on the living person of Jesus, it has no substance and no dynamic force. As soon as Jesus is recognized everything becomes clear. The Gospel ceases to be past history and becomes present fact in which Christ brings an eternal judgment to bear on the events of each day.

Inevitably, this dazzling flash of light which reveals God also reveals to the convert his own personal wretchedness. We shall repeat more than once that the sense of sin comes chiefly not as a piecemeal awareness of sins committed but as a sudden insight: in the presence and the light of God who manifests himself, the person called suddenly sees himself as 'sold to sin'. The authentic revelation of the living God is always accompanied by a revelation of the peculiar misery of man. The two revelations are like two sides of the same medal. Abraham says to God: 'Behold, I have taken upon myself to speak to the Lord, I who am but dust and ashes' (Gen. xviii, 27). Job, with his life shattered by disaster, cannot admit that his misfortunes are the result of his own sins, as his friends try to point out to him. Then God reveals himself and describes his power and his glory to him. And Job exclaims: 'I had heard of thee by the hearing of the ear, but now my eye sees thee; therefore I despise myself, and repent in dust and ashes' (Job xlii, 5-6). Isaiah places himself in the presence of the Lord in all his glory; he hears the angels singing the *Sanctus*. And he cries spontaneously: 'Woe is me! For I am lost; for I am a man of unclean lips . . . for my eyes have seen the King, the Lord of hosts!' (Is. vi, 5). At the sight of the miraculous draft of fishes, Peter discovers at one glance the greatness of Jesus and his own nothingness: 'Depart from me, for I am a sinful man, O Lord' (Luke v, 8).

3. This light on God is at the same time the discovery of a *personal relationship* between the person called and the living God. It is an intuitive discovery whose riches are only perceived little by little in the course of life.

In the Old Testament God gives himself a name, for a name distinguishes a person, or to be more exact gives him an 'existence' in the eyes of those who are invited to use it. The name is only given to enable others to speak it. Thus it is that God, 'He who is', will be 'Yahweh' or 'the Lord' to all those who call on him.[1]

In the New Testament, the Word of God Incarnate receives a name, Jesus, because as the angel says to Joseph, 'he will save his people from their sins' (Matt. i, 21). It is the name by which Christians, saved by Jesus, will call him until the end of time. And through him they learn to know God under a new name full of meaning: father. Through him too they learn the name of the Holy Spirit and discover his divine personality. In the New

---

1. In the Old Testament we find three stages of the revelation of God. For Abraham and the patriarchs he is the 'Most High'. For Moses and the people of Israel he is Yahweh. For Isaiah and the other prophets he is the 'thrice-holy one'.

Testament the personal knowledge of God is differentiated from the knowledge of each one of the three divine persons. We shall deal at length in the final section of this book with the fact that when a Christian begins to distinguish in God each one of the three divine persons and to enter into various relations with them, this is the sign of true conversion and increased faith.

In the presence of the personal God, of the God who bears a name, the person called also receives a name by which God distinguishes him from others and calls him. Abram receives the name Abraham, for, says the Lord, 'I have made you the father of a multitude of nations' (Gen. xvii, 5). God calls Moses by his name (Ex. iii, 4), and to Jeremiah he declares: 'Before I formed you in the womb I knew you' (Jer. i, 5).

Jesus too calls his disciples by their names. Let us recall the varying nuances of friendship revealed in the name Simon, son of John, so often used by Jesus. Christ will later say of himself that he knows each of his sheep by name (John x, 3).

This personal and mutual intimacy between the living God and the person he calls is the first principle of all spiritual growth. When someone discovers that he is personally known to God, and known in a way identical with love, he feels an inexpressible joy like that of being born again, of a great ennoblement with a sense of personal adoption. This is true even of human love, which is a spark of the love of God. When two human beings love each other very deeply their love is mutually creative in a certain sense and makes each one a new person. What, then, must be the effect of the love of God when he calls someone by name? One can understand how the person called yearns for God with a craving which the Bible often compares to thirst.

'As a hart longs for flowing streams,
so longs my soul for thee, O God . . .
My soul thirsts for God, for the living God.
When shall I come and behold the face of God?' (Ps. xlii, 1-2).

'O God, thou art my God, I seek thee,
my soul thirsts for thee; my flesh faints for thee,
as in a dry and weary land where no water is.' (Ps. lxiii, 1).

And Jesus declares himself the object of this desire: 'If any one thirst, let him come to me and drink. He who believes in me, as the scripture has said, "Out of his heart shall flow rivers of living water" ' (John vii, 37-38).

4. This faith is the discovery of the *presence of God* in the heart of man and in the centre of his life. Of course, God is ineffably transcendent, but when he intervenes in the life of someone he calls, he does not remain at a distance as if heaven, where he dwells, were very far away. He makes himself near to them. He says to Abraham: 'Walk before me' (Gen. xvii, 1); to Jeremiah: 'I am with you to deliver you' (Jer. i, 8). With Christ this closeness becomes a true dwelling in the heart of the Christian: 'If a man loves me, he will keep my word, and my Father will love him, and we will come to him and make our home with him' (John xiv, 23), and St Paul tells us that Christ dwells in our hearts through faith (Eph. iii, 17).

5. This discovery of the living and personal God effects a *new birth* in the heart of man (John iii, 3-8).

'By faith, we are born of God himself, and that is why our faith, in its ultimate mystery, evades all natural investigation. Each one of us who believes is a great mystery . . . To us too "it has pleased God to reveal his Son" (Gal. i, 16). It has pleased him. In our faith we live waiting on his good pleasure, which is love. And he wishes us to know it, and in this we shall find our joy.'[1]

Hence, the first element of a growing faith is the ever new discovery of the living God. It is made in one single moment, the moment of conversion. In reality, each day brings a still deeper discovery. And whoever finds God knows full well that everything which God in his love teaches him was contained in the first seed of faith received with the first ray of light.

1. B. M. Chevignard, *La doctrine spirituelle de l'Evangile*, pp. 89-90.

3.

Faith is an Absolute Hope in God to Whom Nothing is Impossible

I. THE HEBREW VERB 'AMAN'

THE meaning of the word 'hope' is explained in the Bible. One might even say that it is God himself who, through the writers of the Bible, invented the word and little by little gave it its content.

As it happens, it is not the noun 'hope' that we find in the Bible but the verb '*aman*', and this is of great significance. A noun translates a concept already developed, and consequently presupposes a whole previous experience, whereas the experience itself, that action of the whole being, is expressed by a verb. In languages which have developed simultaneously with the historical evolution of the peoples who speak them, the verb evolves long before the noun, because these peoples live before they can think; they have experiences before they can analyse them, and the verb enables them to express this experience.

The Hebrew verb *aman* expresses the reaction of someone who believes in God. The word is so full of meaning that we propose to look at it more closely.

1. In the first place *aman* means '*to count on someone who is reliable and strong*'. In this sense it refers to God alone and this is why God is so often called the 'rock'. God is the all-powerful one. Not only has he created everything by his word, but he has only to will something for it to be realized. We have seen this already. Abraham and Mary based their hope on the same key phrase:

13

'with God nothing is impossible'. These words are repeated so often in the Old Testament that Jesus himself uttered them during his agony: 'Abba, Father, all things are possible to thee!' (Mark xiv, 36). Those who are profoundly convinced by them obey blindly. Nothing better shows that obedience than the silence with which Abraham carries out the greater part of God's commands. God is so completely the master and his power so great that Abraham is untroubled by any hesitation, even when it is a matter of sacrificing Isaac.

God values this total obedience very highly, not only because it proves that he who obeys stakes his all on God's word but also because it is a witness in the eyes of all.

We know the story of the waters of Meribah, where Moses had to cope with rebellious people. For years the people of Israel had been marching through the desert towards the promised land, which was still very distant. The problem of water was frequently agonizing. This time it was so terribly serious that the people rose in revolt against Moses. Moses prayed to the Lord, and the glory of God was revealed to him. 'The Lord said to Moses: "Take the rod, and assemble the congregation, you and Aaron your brother, and tell the rock before their eyes to yield its water; so you shall bring water out of the rock for them; so you shall give drink to the congregation and their cattle . . ." And Moses lifted up his hand and *struck the rock with his rod twice;* and water came forth abundantly . . . And the Lord said to Moses and Aaron, "Because you did not believe in me, to sanctify me in the eyes of the people of Israel, therefore you shall not bring this assembly into the land which I have given them" ' (Num. xx, 8-12).

We may be astonished at God's severity towards Moses, who had been absolutely faithful to him all his life. But this very severity makes us understand that hope has no value in the eyes of God unless it is absolute. A hope that is not absolute is too much mingled with human hope. While there is a possibility of succeeding by human means, hope is little more than expectation, a mere caricature of the theological virtue of hope. Human hope does not reckon on God except perhaps in some corner of the conscious. Again, it is a human solution: everything is going badly today, but everything may go well tomorrow. Hope in the biblical sense, on the other hand, only begins where there is no longer any human hope. Divine hope is only built on the ruins of human hope. When it founders it is in God alone that we confide, 'for with him nothing is impossible'.

Jesus takes up the same teaching: 'Have faith in God. Truly, I say to you, whoever says to this mountain, "Be taken up and cast into the sea," and does not doubt in his heart, but believes that what he says will come to pass, it will be done for him' (Mark xi, 22-23). And Jesus demands the same absolute confidence in him: 'Believe in God, believe also in me' (John xiv, 1). Hence, biblical hope is always based on the word of God, the word which is a promise. This promise may refer to an immediate good—a physical miracle or the remission of sin: 'Have confidence, thy sins are forgiven thee.' It may also refer to more distant graces to be fulfilled at the end of time; the coming of the kingdom of God, salvation, the conversion of souls, the gift of heaven. In every case it is a matter of good things which are radically beyond the reach of man and which there is no hope of obtaining by unaided human effort. But by the promise of God, to whom everything is possible, divine hope is possible and can fill the heart and give direction to the whole life.

2. The other meaning of the word *aman* may be expressed as *allowing oneself to be fed by God, leaving oneself in his hands*. Here again the word is rich in the experience of the people of God. From the time the chosen people existed in the person of Abraham and his first descendants, they had been led by God and fed by him, as a flock is led and fed by its shepherd.

The civilization in which the Bible unfolds is a pastoral civilization. Abraham and Moses are shepherds of flocks. When

Samuel goes to the home of Jesse of Bethlehem to find the son whom Yahweh has chosen as king of Israel, the youngest son David is minding the sheep (1 Sam. xvi, 1-13). Absalom, although son of a king, depends for his revenue on raising sheep, and makes the sheep-shearing the occasion of a great feast (2 Sam. xiii, 23-27). The people of Israel therefore have a dual experience: they raise flocks, with all the humble duties this work entails, and they lead a life which is for a long time nomadic, when they are themselves a flock depending on God for their daily needs. Thus they learn in a natural way that the Lord is their shepherd in whom they confide, and by whom they are fed and guided.

'The Lord is my shepherd, I shall not want;
    he makes me lie down in green pastures.
He leads me beside still waters; he restores my soul.
He leads me in paths of righteousness for his name's sake.

Even though I walk through the valley of the shadow of death,
    I fear no evil; for thou art with me;
thy rod and thy staff, they comfort me' (Ps. xxiii, 1-4).

Similarly, the author of Psalm lxxix, 13 says to God: 'We are thy people, the flock of thy pasture.' And in Psalm lxxx he also prays: 'Give ear, O Shepherd of Israel, thou who leadest Joseph like a flock!'

The texts are numerous and eloquent. One could also quote Jeremiah xxiii, 1-5, and above all Ezekiel xxxiv, where God gives himself the characteristics of a shepherd of Israel in words which Jesus uses later in describing himself as the Good Shepherd (John x).

To hope is to allow oneself to be led and sustained by God in total self-abandonment.

II. HOW SHALL WE PROGRESS IN HOPE THROUGHOUT OUR LIFE?

The important thing is to start out on the road with all one's being and all one's life focused on the word of God. Very soon the fundamental question of the collaboration of man's effort and God's omnipotence, or if you like of progress from human to supernatural hope, arises. When a man has heard the word of God, and has discovered the living God, he should find for himself by personal experience, guided by the Holy Spirit, the true relation between his own activity and that of God. That is to say, he should sense in what measure he is collaborating with the omnipotence of God. By this route we can immediately eliminate two extreme errors that lead to a deadlock.

Pelagianism eliminates theological hope in so far as it claims that human effort, the human will, given suitable guidance, is capable of achieving all the supernatural results without the aid of grace. By this hypothesis there is no longer a growth of hope, since there is no supernatural hope. There is only a discipline of the will and a proud awareness of one's own powers.

Quietism, on the other hand, under the pretext of complete abandonment to God, reduces hope to spiritual laziness; man's co-operation is no longer required. Everything comes from God; man has only to receive.

These two deadlocks being eliminated, how is the growth of hope, i.e. the transition from human to supernatural hope, to be effected?

At the outset, man knows what he is striving for and puts all his efforts into it, believing them proportionate to the end in view. Very soon he experiences his weakness, inconstancy and defeats, and has to struggle ceaselessly against the temptation to discouragement or impatience, two subtle expressions of the same pride. If he succeeds in surmounting them and persevering (for humble perseverence is the key which enables him to attain to true hope by degrees), then, without ceasing to renew his co-operation with the grace of God each day, he gradually loses that instinctive attachment to his own virtue and accepts from God the gift of his grace. He progressively loses all hope in himself and places his hope in God. Here below he will never finish that course which St Paul describes more than once:

'But on my own behalf I will not boast, except of my weaknesses . . . And to keep me from being too elated by the abundance of revelations, a thorn was given me in the flesh, a messenger of Satan, to harass me, to keep me from being too elated. Three times I besought the Lord about this, that it should leave me; but he said to me: "My grace is sufficient for you, for my power is made perfect in weakness." I will all the more gladly boast of my weaknesses, that the power of Christ may rest upon me. For the sake of Christ, then, I am content with weaknesses, insults, hardships, persecutions, and calamities; for when I am weak, then I am strong' (2 Cor. xii, 5-10).

'For we know that if the earthly tent we live in is destroyed, we have a building from God, a house not made with hands, eternal in the heavens . . . He who has prepared us for this very thing is God, who has given us the Spirit as a guarantee.

'So we are always of good courage; we know that while we are at home in the body we are away from the Lord, for we walk by faith, not by sight . . . We are of good courage . . .' (2 Cor. v, 5-8).

4.

Faith is Fidelity to God Through Every Trial

> *'Love or respect for truth is traceable to fidelity. Fidelity is linked with a fundamental ignorance of the future . . . When I promise fidelity to someone I do not know what the future holds for us, and it is this very ignorance that gives worth and weight to my promise.'*[1]

WHEN God reveals himself as a living being, man responds by an adherence which commits him for life to a progressive discovery of the face of God.

When God promises every good and confirms his promise by a revelation of his omnipotence, man responds by staking his life on the word of God, with an oblation of total hope and complete self-abandonment.

When, finally, God reveals the faithfulness of his love, man responds with a fidelity forged and tested in surmounting all trials.

These three responses, as we have already said, are but one, and they resolve themselves into a single movement of the soul: the faith of the Bible.

I. WHAT IS FAITHFULNESS?

It is a response to the faithfulness of God. When God chooses and calls someone, he is urged by his love to do so. This love is permanent. God is faithful. He demands of man a similar love and faithfulness. 'Hear, O Israel: The Lord our God is one Lord;

1. Gabriel Marcel, *Being and Having* (London, 1949).

19

and you shall love the Lord your God with all your heart, and
with all your soul, and with all your might' (Deut. vi, 4-5; Matt.
xxii, 37; Mark xii, 29-30; Luke x, 27). The meaning of the word
faithfulness is related to that of charity. But the latter word is
from the New Testament while the word faithfulness is from the
Old Testament, and it shows much more clearly man's slow
progress in responding to God's faithful love. For example, what
does the expression 'to love God with all your might' mean?
How do we really know that all our might is permanently
engaged in this act of love? It is easy to content ourselves with
words when all is going well, or when we are carried away in the
first enthusiasm of conversion. But there are other times, certainly
more numerous and prolonged than these, when we are devoid
of feeling and nothing remains but the heart (in the Gospel sense
of the word), that is to say, our serious will to love. At such times,
can we guarantee that we love with all our might? The fact is
that we can never guarantee this, and such love, or rather faithfulness, is only formed in us by degrees under the action of the
Holy Spirit.

II. THE PATH OF FAITHFULNESS

Let us continue to follow the path of someone who has heard
the call of God and whose life is henceforth pledged to him.

In the first instant he chose God, and this was the starting-
point of his faithfulness. But each day that passes gives him
occasion to choose God anew and thus prove his faithfulness,
which is to last a whole lifetime and which entails a permanent
choosing of God 'above all things'. This unfortunately also
presupposes occasional wavering, choices made against God, and
the whole experience of unfaithfulness. It is the same faithfulness
of God who continues to call and to love that enables man to
start hopefully again in spite of his unfaithfulness the day before.
In order to grow in faithfulness man has to experience his own

unfaithfulness. But this is not enough. God himself, by his Holy Spirit, takes over the direction of this education. To accomplish this, he will use the means which we know from both the Old and the New Testaments, and from the life of every Christian called to faith.

The Bible gives an insight into God's ways in educating his elect in faithfulness. Satan says to God of Job:

'Does Job fear God for naught? Hast thou not put a hedge about him and his house and all that he has, on every side? . . . But put forth thy hand now, and touch all that he has, and he will curse thee to thy face' (Job i, 9-11).

'My son, if you come forward to serve the Lord, prepare yourself for temptation. Set your heart right and be steadfast, and do not be hasty in time of calamity . . . Accept whatever is brought upon you, and in changes that humble you be patient. For gold is tested in the fire, and acceptable men in the furnace of humiliation' (Ecclus. ii, 1-5).

1. *The Duration.* The passing of time, but still more the slowness of time, is a great teacher of faithfulness. It is easy to be faithful for a day or a week, but when it goes on for years, and the monotony of the days becomes burdensome, faithfulness becomes more painful to maintain. For it is no longer sustained by the ardour born of a rigorous but transitory encounter.

2. *The Desert.* In the Bible it was the desert of sand that Moses and his people had to cross, with all the dangers and difficulties of such an adventure. But it is also the spiritual desert that comes from the apparent silence of God. And all who wish to be faithful to God have to cross this desert once or many times. The Bible makes us listen to Job's lamentations and the cry of the suffering servant: 'My God, my God, why hast thou forsaken me?' (Ps. xxii, 1), which Jesus repeats on the cross.

3. *Persecution and Suffering.* Here again is a universal experience of which the Bible tells us, and which we know from life itself.

Abraham knew the suffering of having to sacrifice his only son Isaac, and he consented to it without renouncing his faithfulness to God. The suffering which in the Old Testament was pure proof of God's love has become, since the death and the resurrection of Jesus, a participation in the redemption of the world.

No one who has not been initiated into the agony of Jesus in Gethsemane and his abandonment on the cross can have an inkling of what faithfulness means. As St Paul says so emphatically, we must know Christ crucified. It is St Paul too who expresses most clearly the Christian's first experience of participating in his Lord's passion:

'But as servants of God we commend ourselves in every way: through great endurance in afflictions, hardships, calamities, beatings, imprisonments, tumults, labours, watching, hunger ... We are treated as impostors, and yet are true ...' (2 Cor. vi, 4–9).

'I have great confidence in you; I have great pride in you; I am filled with comfort. With all our afflictions, I am overjoyed. For even when we came into Macedonia, our bodies had no rest but we were afflicted at every turn—fighting without and fear within' (2 Cor. vii, 4–5).

'Now you have observed my teaching', writes St Paul to Timothy, '. . . my faith, my patience, my love, my steadfastness, my persecutions, my sufferings, what befell me at Antioch, at Iconium, and at Lystra, what persecutions I endured; yet from them all the Lord rescued me. Indeed all who desire to live a godly life in Christ Jesus will be persecuted' (2 Tim. iii, 10–12).

All these trials train the Christian in faithfulness by obliging him not only to overcome self but also to unite himself to the mystery of the cross of Christ. He is thus given the opportunity of humbly experiencing his solidarity with the multitudes in the world who suffer physically or in their hearts without knowing that they are co-operating in the passion of the Lord. In the second epistle to the Corinthians, St Paul enumerates his vicissitudes at length—the persecutions he has suffered, the dangers he has passed through; and recalling his anxieties about all the Christian communities, he adds: 'Who is weak, and I am not weak? Who is made to fall, and I am not indignant?' (2 Cor. xi, 29).

We must repeat that fidelity to God can only be proved by continual trials, desolation and suffering. It is thus that, by union with the passion of Christ and participation in the sufferings of the world, the Christian gradually discovers a new face of Christ. At the beginning of his real life of conversion he cannot know if he will be faithful. At the end of his life, having been tested for a long time like metal in a furnace, he can thank the Lord for having sustained him in spite of the weakness of which he is calmly convinced. His faithfulness derives from the faithfulness of God and this is why it has become unshakable.

II
Abraham's Faith

Introduction

ABRAHAM holds a vital place in the Bible. No one is mentioned more often, not only in the Old Testament but also in the New Testament. Nevertheless, there are few biblical characters about whom we know less and have less human detail. Let us compare Abraham with David, for instance. The character of David is clearly delineated; we can get a clear mental picture of the king, both his person and his character. Of Abraham, on the other hand, we are not given any description of this kind. His portrait is stylized. He is nothing but a response to a call; he is only a 'yes' said to God. He is the man of faith, and that *par excellence*. Everything else about him is unimportant and can remain in the shade; and what we are told of his life has but one purpose: to make his heroic faith stand out in relief. 'Abraham believed.' What more is there to say?

Nevertheless one objection springs to our minds. If the character of Abraham is so simple, how can we perceive a growth in his faith? How can we find in his life an example and a light for our own path through life?

Though Abraham's spiritual character is so very simple and stable, his example can show us how spontaneous and dynamic an act of faith can be. The events of his life enable us to distinguish clearly the means which God employs to push hope and fidelity to their utmost limits.

It is this very simplicity in the character of Abraham that has made him the focus of endless reflection. His history has been recalled and meditated upon by the Jews hundreds and thousands of times. The whole of the Old Testament is a tireless reiteration of the simple story of a call of God and of Abraham's response. Each generation has discovered new marvels in this meditation,

27

and the sacred writers from century to century have dwelt ever more deeply on the lesson of that first event.

The New Testament too contributes its stone to the edifice. Zechariah and Mary, in their canticles, recall the promise made by God to Abraham. Jesus speaks frequently of the patriarch, and on reading the fourth chapter of the epistle to the Romans and the eleventh chapter of the epistle to the Hebrews, we notice that the apostle, continuing the rabbinical teaching, is inspired by the example of Abraham in his descriptions of the dimensions of faith.

We may say that the whole spiritual substance of the faithful Israelite is embodied in Abraham. We may also say that the whole history of the Church is contained in him as it were in embryo.

Finally, we may say that the discovery of God which each converted person makes when he first sees the light not only reproduces the first revelation made by God to Abraham but actually rests on it as on a rock. We may recall Pascal's famous 'God of Abraham, God of Isaac, God of Jacob . . . God of Jesus Christ. Total and sweet renunciation.' Abraham was the first man since the Fall to enter into personal and mutual communication with God. True, Enoch had 'walked with God' before him, and Noah had received a clear mission at the time of the Flood. But Abraham was the first to be taken hold of by God for a spiritual destiny and to give his response by his faith. All those who since then have known God, heard his voice and responded by pledging their lives to him, are sons of Abraham. 'For he is the father of us all' says St Paul (Rom. iv, 16).

5.

Abraham Discovers the Living God

ABRAHAM is the man to whom God spoke, who took heed of God's words and responded to God. In this dialogue God took the initiative, and there is no proof that Abraham had merited this privilege by previous virtues, or that he had any claim to preference above other members of his family, his brothers Nahor or Haran for instance. God intervenes freely and gratuitously. And he intervenes often. We read frequently of his doing so in one way or another—'the Lord said to Abraham! . . .', 'the word of the Lord was addressed to Abraham . . .', 'the Lord appeared to Abraham and said to him . . .', etc. This is why Abraham acted with such obedience. He was certain that God was guiding his life, and this was the meaning of all his actions.

Nothing is less abstract than this revelation of himself which God makes to Abraham. He makes himself recognized by recalling his previous interventions: 'I am the Lord who brought you from Ur of the Chaldeans' (Gen. xv, 7). He says of himself: 'I am God Almighty' (Gen. xvii, 1). He carries on a familiar dialogue with him (Gen. xviii, 17-33). He calls him by name: 'Abraham', and the latter replies: 'Here am I.'

There is such intimacy between God and his chosen one that Abraham's personal knowledge of God will be the source of the faith of all his descendants. For the Israelites God will never be an abstract divinity without face or voice. He will be the God of Abraham, he who has a countenance and who speaks. The very expression 'God of Abraham' has something possessive about it, something familiar, concrete and almost tangible.

This God who is so near reveals himself at the same time as the transcendent God. We know the episode of Melchizedek, king of

Salem, he who was 'priest of God Most High'. He blessed Abraham and said:

'Blessed be Abram by God Most High, maker of heaven and earth; and blessed be God Most High, who has delivered your enemies into your hand!' (Gen. xiv, 19-20).

Let us understand the significance of this episode. Melchizedek and Abraham worship God Most High while their neighbours and their families worship the moon, or the sun, or a tree, or a spring. Abraham's ancestors, for instance, worshipped the moon, and the majority of the tribes in the region were sun worshippers. Before his meeting with Melchizedek, Abraham had been moved by God, but at that time he was still incapable of calling God by name. Melchizedek plays somewhat the same role in relation to Abraham as John the Baptist in relation to the disciples of Jesus and Jesus himself. He explains and shows the way. He perceives that this transcendent God whose priest he is ('Blessed be Abram by God Most High, maker of heaven and earth'), is also the God who intervenes in history and events ('Blessed be God Most High, who has delivered your enemies into your hands!'). Henceforth, for Abraham and for all who come after him, God is at once the Most High and he who reveals himself, acting among them. Here is the remote preparation for the incarnation. Centuries will pass and will lead up to the revelation of Immanuel—'God with us' (Is. vii, 14), and finally of 'the Word of God made flesh'.

'The essential characteristics of the God of biblical tradition, his transcendence and immanence in a supernatural history, are already acquired, and henceforward, in all that is to come of that history, each time God intervenes in an event of that history, he will reveal himself a little more while revealing his own design in and through events.

'Thus there will be a progressive revelation of God linked up with the successive initiatives on the part of God until finally he is to appear personally in that history, to be for ever God with us: Jesus Christ.'[1]

The Melchizedek episode is decisive for Abraham because immediately after this meeting we find him invoking 'God Most High, maker of heaven and earth' (Gen. xiv, 22), like Melchizedek.

This is the name that Abraham gives from now onwards to the God who has intervened in his life and who is the object of his faith. He is at once God Most High and the one who calls him, his guide in an unknown adventure, accepted with hope.

1. R. P. Feret, 'Bible et Education', *Proceedings of the Congress of Teaching Nuns* (July 1953), p. 47.

6.

Abraham Stakes His Life on God's Word

OF all the aspects of Abraham's faith, it is his hope which has most impressed his descendants. It has always been the subject of meditation and was undoubtedly an essential element of rabbinical teaching in the time of Christ. We have a convincing indication of this in the introduction of such catechesis into the New Testament by St Paul in the epistle to the Romans, and by the author of the epistle to the Hebrews, both authors being doctors of the Law. 'And I will make of you a great nation, and I will bless you, and make your name great, so that you will be a blessing. I will bless those who bless you, and him who curses you I will curse; and by you all the families of the earth shall bless themselves' (Gen. xii, 2-3).

The name of Abraham will serve as a blessing not only for those of his own race but also for 'those who bless' him, that is to say, those who continue his mission and his hope in the Lord.

I. WHY HAS ABRAHAM SUCH CONFIDENCE IN GOD?

First, because *God has revealed himself to him in such an overwhelming light* that he surrenders himself to his guidance. 'By faith Abraham obeyed when he was called to go out to a place which he was to receive as an inheritance; and he went out, not knowing where he was to go' (Heb. xi, 8).

Secondly, it is because *that call contains a dual promise:*

(a) A promise due for fulfilment relatively soon, and clearly temporal: 'And I will give to you, and to your descendants after you, the land of your sojournings, all the land of Canaan, for an everlasting possession; and I will be their God' (Gen. xvii, 8); 'I will make your descendants as the dust of the earth' (Gen. xiii, 16).

(b) A spiritual and eschatological promise, based on the preceding one, and lasting until the end of time: 'I will indeed bless you, and I will multiply your descendants as the stars of heaven . . . And your descendants shall possess the gate of their enemies, and by your descendants shall all the nations of the earth bless themselves, because you have obeyed my voice' (Gen. xxii, 17-18).

These promises feed the minds of generations of Israelites for at the dawn of the New Testament we find Zechariah and Mary, devout Israelites brought up on the Bible, recalling the promise made to Abraham and applying it to themselves. Mary says: 'He has helped his servant Israel, in remembrance of his mercy, as he spoke to our fathers, to Abraham and to his posterity for ever' (Luke i, 54-55). Zechariah, in his turn, rejoices at God's remembrance of 'his holy covenant, the oath that he swore to our father Abraham' (Luke i, 72-73).

In the calling of Abraham we can recognize the characteristic features of every divine vocation. If he has been chosen, it is not for himself alone, but for others. If he is blessed by the Lord, it is in order that all who live in his spirit and follow his example may be blessed. His vocation is a 'missionary' vocation in the sense that all the nations of the earth are to be raised up as if by leaven because they come from the seed that the call of God has sown in him. If Abraham's posterity in the flesh is blessed it is so that all races may be blessed through it. 'There will therefore be a double posterity, that of the flesh and that of the spirit, the first subordinate to the second.'[1] All future vocations are to find in the example of Abraham their universal dimensions. The acceptance of Mary's consent is explicitly linked up with Abraham. And one can even say that the preaching of the Gospel to the ends

1. Lécuyer, *Abraham, notre Pere*, p. 20.

of the earth stems from Abraham's setting out for a missionary destiny.

Finally, it is because Abraham knows that with God nothing is impossible. The epistle to the Romans and the epistle to the Hebrews abound in pregnant and striking examples of this:

'For he (Abraham) is the father of us all . . . in the presence of the God in whom he believed, *who gives life to the dead and calls into existence the things that do not exist* . . . He did not weaken in faith when he considered his own body, which was as good as dead because he was about a hundred years old, or when he considered the barrenness of Sarah's womb. No distrust made him waver concerning the promise of God, but he grew strong in his faith as he gave glory to God, fully convinced that God was able to do what he had promised' (Rom. iv, 16-21).

'Now faith is the assurance of things hoped for, the conviction of things not seen . . . By faith Abraham obeyed when he was called to go out to a place which he was to receive as an inheritance; *and he went out, not knowing where he was to go.* By faith he sojourned in the land of promise, as in a foreign land . . . For he looked forward to the city which has foundations, whose builder and maker is God . . . By faith Abraham, when he was tested, offered up Isaac, and he who had received the promises was ready to offer up his only son, of whom it was said, "Through Isaac shall your descendants be named." *He considered that God was able to raise men even from the dead'* (Heb. xi, 8-9, 17-19).

When hope is founded on such convictions it has an extraordinary dynamic force, and God can do great things through one who surrenders himself to him in this way.

II. HOW DID GOD PUT ABRAHAM'S HOPE TO THE TEST?

We said above that Abraham's hope was so strong and firmly

founded from the beginning that it did not have to grow. However, it had to last a lifetime and be put to the test in order to attain that strength and stability which alone ensure perseverance. It was necessary, in the first place, for Abraham to accept the divine promises and receive them into his heart so that they would have time to mature there. The promises of God then became the object of Abraham's meditation, and of the meditation of all his descendants. The Bible is nothing more than a record of the acceptance and meditation of the divine promises, and it bears witness to an ever deeper understanding of their range.

But it was still necessary that the education given by God should presuppose in Abraham's heart all the natural efforts that could serve as human support to his supernatural hope—every human opportunity of coming through without divine intervention. That is why God began to call Abraham when he was already eighty years of age, and when his wife Sarah, who had never borne him any children, was also advanced in years. And it was to this old couple that God promised posterity. Then he left them worried and troubled for twenty years more before renewing his promise and finally giving them their son Isaac. 'Therefore from one man, and him as good as dead, were born descendants as many as the stars of heaven and as the innumerable grains of sand by the seashore' (Heb. xi, 12).

Truly, as St Paul says in his own way in the epistle to the Romans, Abraham's supernatural hope is born of the death of human hope. 'In hope he believed against hope' (Rom. iv, 18).

And when Isaac was growing up God demanded of Abraham that he should sacrifice him. Abraham, without a moment's hesitation, set out to do this, for his hope was in a different sphere and on a different level from human hope. He knew that God was 'able to raise men even from the dead' (Heb. xi, 19). And the sacred writer goes on to say that all this is a lesson for us.

St Francis de Sales writes:

'The saints all praise the virtues of Abraham. St Paul gives him the most praise since "in hope he believed against hope itself". God had promised him that his posterity would be multiplied as the stars of the sky and the sand of the sea, and yet he received the commandment to kill his son Isaac. But the humble Abraham did not lose hope; rather, he hoped against hope itself even to the point of obeying the commandment of God to kill his son. God, however, did not hold him to his word. And so Abraham's hope was truly great, for he could see nothing to which he could hold but God's word which had been given to him.

'What a true and solid foundation is the word of God, for it is infallible! Abraham sets out with unparalleled simplicity to do God's will. He does not wait to reflect or to reply when God commands him to leave the land of his people and go to a place which he will show him but which he does not specify; this is so that Abraham may embark all the more simply on the barque of his Divine Providence.'[1]

1. St Francis de Sales, *Entretiens spirituels* (entr. VI, 'de l'Espérance').

7.

Abraham Proves His Faithfulness by Overcoming All the Trials God Sends Him

I. UPROOTED FROM HIS PAST

THE first trial God gives Abraham to bear is being uprooted from his past, his country and his family. The first word God says to Abraham is 'Go!' 'Go from your country and your kindred and your father's house to the land that I will show you' (Gen. xii, 1). God obliges him to change the course of his life radically. The obstacle of advanced age, and that of family bonds—so close in the East—are treated as unimportant by God. We must admit, however, that Abraham endured these things, no doubt with grief and torn human feelings. So here we find him venturing out onto unknown ways, full of dangers which he could not fail to foresee, bound for an unknown destination and a country which he was never to know. 'And he went out, knowing not where he was to go . . . he sojourned in the land of promise as in a foreign land . . . These all died in faith, not having received what was promised' (Heb. xi, 8-13).

Abraham may not have been a nomad by origin. The excavations made in his country, Ur of the Chaldees, reveal that at the time of his departure, about 2000 B.C., that region had an urban civilization. Abraham may well have taken to a nomad life from time to time through force of circumstances. But we do well to emphasize the psychological importance of his departure from Ur. In leaving his original milieu, his country, his family, and in changing his way of life, Abraham frees himself to become

37

wholly at God's disposal. He leaves the level of worldly things to advance to a higher level, that of the divine will.

'He left one thing, his worldly wisdom, and took on another thing, faith. Otherwise he would have realized the absurdity of the journey, and not set out at all.'[1]

II. THE TRIAL OF THE DESERT

After the initial trial of uprooting, God imposes the trial of the desert. He says: 'Go to the land that I will show you.' It is hard to leave one's country, and to be on the road for the rest of one's life without ever arriving at one's destination. Where am I bound for? What am I to do next? How long shall I be away? Abraham could not fail to ask himself these questions, which remained unanswered, and to suffer agonies in the silence.

God commands, so one must obey. The peculiar trial of travelling through a desert is not knowing the route, the stages or the end, and never being able to take one's bearings or ascertain where one is on the mysterious journey. Hardest of all is never to see fulfilled the promises in which one has believed. God had said to Abraham: 'For all the land which you see I will give to you' (Gen. xiii, 15). Of this promised land, Abraham had only a cave and a piece of ground in which to bury his wife, and this he had to buy from the native people. The writer of the epistle to the Hebrews describes in superb words the deep motive of Abraham's faithfulness in the barren desert:

'For he looked forward to the city which has foundations, whose builder and maker is God . . . These all died in faith, not having received what was promised, but having seen it and greeted it from afar, and having acknowledged that they were strangers and exiles on the earth. For people who speak thus make it clear that they are seeking a homeland . . . But as it is, they desire a better country, that is, a heavenly one. There-

1. Kierkegaard, *Fear and Trembling,* London, 1939.

fore God is not ashamed to be called their God, for he has prepared for them a city' (Heb. xi, 10-16).

III. THE TEST OF TIME

Alongside the trial of the desert, Abraham endures the test of time. God promises Abraham that he will have a son, and this first promise is made when he is eighty years of age. But twenty years are to pass before Abraham hears that the promise is at last to be realized (Gen. xvii, 4-8). Meanwhile each passing year makes the realization of the prophecy seem more improbable. Nothing is easier than to express, in a single sentence, the duration of time passed; but it is unspeakably hard to pass that time waiting for the issue that never comes. And during these twenty years the Lord seldom comes to sustain Abraham in his faithfulness. There is no test of faithfulness more wearing than length of time and monotony of days, and nothing more dreary than the constant struggle against the wearing down of the will which the daily round imposes.

The sacred test gives an extremely sober account of the anxieties and the normal psychological reactions of this period. On one occassion, however, they do come to light, in a dialogue between God and Abraham. After the episode of the victory over the kings and the interventions of the king of Sodom and of Melchizedek, God comes to encourage his servant: 'Fear not, Abram, I am your shield; your reward shall be very great' (Gen. xv, 1). For the first time Abraham emerges from his silence and replies to God. Perhaps he is encouraged by the name of God Most High which Melchizedek has just disclosed to him and which enables him to enter into a dialogue with God. 'But Abram said, "O Lord God, what wilt thou give me, for I continue childless, and the heir of my house is Eliezer of Damascus?" And Abram said, "Behold, thou hast given me no offspring; and a slave born in my house will be my heir" ' (Gen. xv, 2-3).

This response may be interpreted as the expression of a complaint and of anxiety regarding the seriousness of God's promises. But it may also be interpreted as a sign of 'the perfect confidence of Abraham face to face with his God; he bares his soul to him in all simplicity, showing him his sorrows. The only reward that would please him on this earth would be to have a child in whom he would begin to see the fulfilment of the promise; any other riches that God might grant him would go to strangers . . .'.[1] Abraham speaks to God as one speaks to a friend, hiding from him none of his thoughts.

Abraham's confident question recalls the question that his distant descendant Mary is to ask the Angel Gabriel: 'How can this be, since I have no husband?' (Luke i, 34). God responds to Abraham's confidence with an explicit promise: 'This man shall not be your heir; your own son shall be your heir' (Gen. xv, 4). But Abraham has not yet come to the end of his waiting, and he will have to wait many years more to see the promise realized, yet even so he will remain faithful.

IV. THE TEST OF BLOOD

'After these things God tested Abraham, and said to him, "Abraham!"' (Gen. xxii, 1). It is no longer circumstances that are to test Abraham, but God himself. All the dialogue that follows is clearly separate from the impersonal and purely narrative character of the other chapters of Genesis. An emotion which is hardly suppressed animates every sentence relating this episode.

Abraham replies: 'Here am I', with a readiness and simplicity which bear witness to his faith and suppleness in the hands of God. And God says: 'Take your son, your only son Isaac, whom you love, and go to the land of Moriah, and offer him there as a

1. Lécuyer, *Abraham, notre Père*, pp. 64–65, commenting on St John Chrysostom's Homily.

burnt offering upon one of the mountains of which I shall tell you' (Gen. xxii, 2).

Such is God's hard, even cruel decision. 'God seems to take pleasure in piling up words into a kind of litany of tenderness to rend the heart of the patriarch: "Your son, your only son Isaac, whom you love".'[1]

The story that follows unfolds with a simplicity and at times a poignant, unspoken emotion which one can sense beneath the words: 'So Abraham rose early in the morning, saddled his ass, and took two of his young men with him, and his son Isaac; and he cut the wood for the burnt offering, and arose and went to the place of which God had told him' (Gen. xxii, 3). No detail emphasizing the almost everyday simplicity of the action is omitted: getting up early, saddling the ass for the journey; the servants and the child helping in the preparations for the day that is beginning; the wood being cut for the burnt offering. Each word has its significance; we are present at the scene. The journey lasts three days.[2]

'On the third day Abraham lifted up his eyes and saw the place afar off.' The story is soberly told, but to appreciate Abraham's faithfulness we must put ourselves in his place and live those three days in the agony and suspense of the inescapable climax. 'Then Abraham said to his young men, "Stay here with the ass; I and the lad will go yonder and worship, and come back again to you." ' Abraham wants to be alone when consummating the sacrifice that is asked of him.[3] Would he have had the strength to carry it out before others?

Origen, commenting on some words in the epistle to the Hebrews—'He considered that God was able to raise men even from the dead; hence, figuratively speaking, he did receive him

1. Lécuyer, *op. cit.,* p. 118.
2. The pilgrimage of Jesus to Jerusalem with Mary and Joseph was also to last three days.
3. Later, Jesus would prefer to pray in solitude at certain decisive stages of his life.

back' (Heb. xi, 19)—thinks that Abraham's declaration to his servants proves that he believed his son would be raised from the dead. He says in effect to his servants: '*We will go* yonder and worship, after which *we shall come back* again to you.' We must definitely exclude the possibility that Abraham wished to deceive his servants in telling them that he would come back with the child when he well knew that he was going to sacrifice him. It must be admitted that during those three days before the sacrifice Abraham pondered every one of God's words. There were the words promising him countless descendants: 'for through Isaac shall your descendants be named.' But then there was also the command to offer Isaac in sacrifice: 'Offer him there as a burnt offering upon one of the mountains of which I shall tell you.' As God cannot lie or contradict himself, there is only one solution to the dilemma. After Isaac has been sacrificed, God will raise the child to life again. 'He considered that God was able to raise men even from the dead; hence, figuratively speaking, he did receive him back' (Heb. xi, 19).

'And Abraham took the wood of the burnt offering, and laid it on Isaac his son; and he took in his hand the fire and the knife. So they went both of them together.' Then follows a dialogue of such stark simplicity and restrained tenderness that we cannot fail to be moved by it.

'And Isaac said to his father Abraham, "My father!" And he said, "Here am I, my son."

'He said, "Behold, the fire and the wood; but where is the lamb for a burnt offering?"

'Abraham said, "God will provide himself the lamb for a burnt offering, my son."

'So they went both of them together' (Gen. xxii, 7-8).

The terseness of the sentences hardly conceals the father's emotion and tenderness, nor the affectionate confidence of the child. This scene is profoundly human because of the value of the sentiments expressed in it.

'God will provide', says Abraham. The patriarch has placed himself with blind confidence in the hands of God. We glimpse in outline another father who sacrifices another son. Isaac represents Christ. In the two episodes of which the first outlines the second the two victims go through the same actions. Both are a sacrifice in the hands of their fathers. Both are loaded with the wood for the sacrifice. This episode unfolds in the same region, for Mount Moriah is the hill on which Solomon was later to erect the Temple of the Lord. And the words of Abraham to Isaac, 'God will provide', presage the day when God himself will provide the lamb for sacrifice in giving his Son, the Lamb of God.

'When they came to the place of which God had told him, Abraham built an altar there, and laid the wood in order, and bound Isaac his son, and laid him on the altar, upon the wood. Then Abraham put forth his hand, and took the knife to slay his son. But the angel of the Lord called to him from heaven, and said, "Abraham, Abraham!" And he said, "Here am I". He said, "Do not lay your hand upon the lad or do anything to him; for now I know that you fear God, seeing you have not withheld your son, your only son, from me" ' (Gen. xxii, 9-12).

St Paul was later to take up these words in referring to God himself, 'who did not spare his own Son but gave him up for us all' (Rom. viii, 32).

'Thus Abraham becomes the image of the eternal Father sacrificing his Son for the salvation of man; that which God did not permit his servant to carry out, he himself ultimately carried out in delivering his beloved Son to death.'[1]

The conclusion of the incident connects us directly with Abraham's sacrifice by making us share its benefits. 'And by

1. Lécuyer, *op. cit.,* p. 124.

your descendants shall all the nations of the earth bless themselves, because you have obeyed my voice' (Gen. xxii, 18).

The spiritual repercussions of Abraham's sacrifice of Isaac will last to the end of time, for the salvation of all mankind stems from the patriarch's obedience. We get a glimpse in it of the broad outlines of the divine plan of salvation whereby the disobedience of Adam will one day be atoned for by the obedience of the Son of God Incarnate. 'For as by one man's disobedience many were made sinners, so by one man's obedience many will be made righteous' (Rom. v, 19).

God's plan is marvellously simple. He gives us the initial outline of it in Abraham's consent to sacrifice his son Isaac. He realizes it in his own Son by not hesitating to sacrifice him. Finally, he associates us with the redemption of the world in the measure that, by our obedience, we faithfully accept God's plan for us.

Conclusion

LET us try to arrive at the gist of Abraham's faith, which we have been endeavouring to analyse in this section. There are two expressions in holy scripture which enable us to do this.

Three times the Bible describes Abraham as '*the friend*' of God (Is. xli, 8). Abraham is he to whom God spoke and who knew God personally in a dialogue which gradually became confident and friendly. God's presence became as familiar to him as that of someone who resided under the same roof and completely shared his life. Abraham, the friend of God, had confidence in his friend. 'In hope he believed against hope' and was 'fully convinced that God was able to do what he had promised' (Rom. iv, 18, 21). He staked his life on the word of God.

Abraham, the friend of God, was faithful to this friendship, and his love was so strong that at a crucial moment in his life he did not hesitate to sacrifice his deepest human affections to it. We can see the depth and force of Abraham's act of faith: it dominated his whole existence and stretched his hope and faithfulness to the utmost. It was not an intellectual act but a total commitment of the heart, an impetus that came from the core of his being; it was the faith of a friend in a friend.

The other expression which characterizes Abraham is that of *father*: 'Abraham the father of us all' (Rom. iv, 16). He it was who begot not only that vast race from which Christ came but also all those who, like him, stake their lives on the word of God.

We are allied to Abraham by our faith and through him to the heavenly Father, of whom Abraham is at once the friend and the symbol. Moreover, according to Jesus, the reward of heaven will include closeness to Abraham. The wicked rich man sees Lazarus 'in the bosom of Abraham' (Luke xvi, 22), that is, in the place of honour by Abraham's side.

III

The Faith of Mary

'I am the handmaid of the Lord.'
(Luke i, 38).

8.

The Spirit in which to Approach this Meditation

I. THE SIMPLICITY OF GOD'S PLAN

MARY, like Abraham, certainly has an unusual destiny, but if we see her only under this aspect we are liable to be discouraged and fail to see how she can possibly serve as an example for us. The truth is that she is at once unique and like the rest of us.

What is God's plan for Mary according to the scriptures? For God certainly has a plan for her. That is to say, he has given her a role in the salvation of the world, just as he gave one to Abraham and also reserves for each of us an irreplaceable function in the plan of redemption.

The search for God's plan for Mary, as the Bible reveals it to us, not only makes clear the basis of a valid Mariology, but also reveals, in her spiritual journey, the decisive lines in the growth of every vocation.

If it is true that each soul has a vocation proper to itself, and that the Holy Spirit is inventive enough to trace out a particular route for it, it is no less certain that all vocations grow according to the same laws and pass through identical stages. It is a great joy to the mind to discover the admirable simplicity of God's plan and to recognize the same broad outlines of this plan, not only in the history of the people of Israel and of the Church but also in the spiritual path of Abraham, of Mary, and of any Christian.

II. MARY AT THE CROSSROADS BETWEEN THE OLD AND THE NEW TESTAMENTS

When a convert enters the Catholic Church, he finds himself

suddenly faced with a highly elaborate Marian theology and cult. He is very often disconcerted by this teaching, presented *en bloc* with no apparent roots in the Bible.

Such converts are more numerous than one would think. They came up against the living God at some turn in their path through life. They have become capable of grasping at a glance the simplicity of God's plan for Mary, since they grasp intuitively the simplicity of God's plan for themselves. Moreover, they have a particular aptitude for reading the Bible and finding in it the main outlines of the divine plan.

In this they show themselves more penetrating than cradle Catholics educated in the faith. But Christians both old and new are equally ignorant when they read the liturgical texts which the Church has chosen for Mary's feasts. For the greater number of them, what significance has the Church's application to Mary of passages from the book of Wisdom, when there seems to outward appearing to be such contempt of the literal meaning of the texts used? What do invocations in the Litany of our Lady such as 'Mirror of Justice', 'Seat of Wisdom', 'Ark of the Covenant' mean to them? Are they not tempted to believe that the sound of the words hides the empty or esoteric nature of the thought, or that oriental lyricism cannot be assimilated by their western minds? However, for some years past, the door has been wide open to progress. The New Testament in particular is becoming more and more the spiritual food of modern Catholics. They are placing their confidence more and more in the word of God, and are seeking a vital and direct contact with it by reading the New Testament in the Church. Does not the word of God always produce faith and bring grace to those who allow it to evoke a response in their hearts as if it were being addressed personally to them there and then?

The New Testament reveals only part of its riches to those who do not know the Old Testament and who separate these two complementary stages of divine revelation.

All through the Old Testament a body of revelation concerning Mary and the mystery surrounding her takes the form of themes woven into the texture of the history. We shall confine ourselves to listing them: daughter of Zion, ark of the covenant, wisdom of God, spouse of Yahweh, woman, or new Eve. These themes, scattered throughout the sacred books and intermingled one with another, converge on Mary and enable us to understand her life and role.[1] It is impossible really to understand the stories of the annunciation and the visitation in St. Luke if we do not know that St Luke is alluding very clearly to the ark of the covenant, which Mary represents for him (Luke i, 35, 42). Similarly, it is impossible really to understand the episodes of the marriage feast of Cana and of Mary at the foot of the cross unless we remember that St John's narratives are a continuation of the theme of the new Eve (John ii, 4; xix, 2-6).[2] Mary, symbol of the Church, stands like the Church at the meeting-point of the Old and New Testaments. In her turn, she becomes the point of departure for a full reflection, a complete theological development. In her we can discern the Church, and the development of Marian doctrine is closely related to the development of our faith within the Church.[3]

Let us put ourselves in the place of a Christian at the end of the first century. Let us suppose him to be a Jew by race and a rabbi by training, like Paul, Apollos and so many others. He knows the Old Testament thoroughly, not only word for word and almost by heart, but also in synthesis. He has seen the admirable simplicity of God's plan expressed in the themes which run through all the books (the canticles of Zechariah, Mary and

1. Bouyer, L., *Man and Woman with God. An Essay on the place of the Virgin Mary in Christian Theology* (London, 1960).
2. Laurentin, R., *Structure et Théologie de Luc I et II* (Paris, 1957); Braun, *La Mère des Fidèles* (Tournai, 1954).
3. It is the Church which comes first. All that is said of the Church has been perfectly achieved in Mary who was herself alone, in a certain way, the complete Church, whether at Cana where she was in advance of the apostles in faith, or again now when she is in advance of us in the matter of glory.

Simeon, for instance, give a true idea of this overall understanding of the Old Testament possessed by those who lived at the dawn of the New Testament). This Jewish Christian had been present when the Gospel was first spreading. In his eyes the books of the New Testament have a different character from the character they have for us. He had heard the Gospels preached long before he had read the texts, if indeed he had read them. In any case he did not have the sacred books complete and in the permanent order in which we know them now. But—and this is especially important—he had grasped by experience what we find so hard to understand, namely that the New Testament is thoroughly rooted in the old, so much so indeed that it can only be read properly in the light of the latter: *Novum Testamentum in Vetere latet.* It is this knowledge of the totality of the divine message that Mary possessed, and in so far as certain texts in the New Testament which speak of her come from her own memories, we can recognize the signs of this knowledge in them.

III. MARY IN THE NEW TESTAMENT

The New Testament texts were written in a chronological order very different from that in which we find them today. This is of great importance in everything that touches Mary.

The Christian of today gets the impression that Mary enters very little into the New Testament. There are the first two chapters of St Matthew, a few lines in St Mark, the first two chapters of St Luke, and the episodes of the marriage feast of Cana and at the foot of the cross in St John's Gospel. Her name is mentioned only once in the Acts, and in all the epistles there is but one allusion to her (Gal. iv, 4). This unfortunate impression is intensified by the fact that these rare mentions of Mary more often than not put her in the shade, if not in an unfavourable or painful position.

Here again, if we are to understand these very meaningful

texts, we must put ourselves in the place of a Jewish Christian of
the first century at the time when the books of the New Testament were one after another coming into being. The most
ancient documents are the discourses of St Peter recounted in the
Acts of the Apostles, which St Luke, the author of the Acts,
obviously reproduced from manuscript notes, without taking the
trouble to rewrite them in his own style. We find in these
discourses the apostles' catechetical teaching in its original form:
'Men of Judea, you await the Messiah on the faith of the prophets.
This Messiah has come: he is Jesus of Nazareth whom you
crucified. But God raised him up, as we have witnessed, and he
made him both Lord and Christ.' Here we have the gist of all
early apostolic preaching. This forms the basis of the epistles of
St Paul which are the most ancient books of the New Testament.
It illuminates the other epistles, as well as the first Gospels (Mark
in its entirety, Matthew and Luke from their third chapters
onwards). All these writings originated before the years 60-70,
but the discourses which they reproduce were repeated orally
from the year of the death, resurrection and ascension of Jesus
until they came to be written down. And the lack of information
about Mary in these writings should not surprise us.

It was not only that she had no part in the basic argumentation
summarized above and addressed to the Jews who were awaiting
the Messiah, but also that she was still alive at the time of this
preaching. Her function in the Church was fulfilled solely by her
silent and prayerful presence, which the author of the Acts lets us
perceive (Acts i, 14).

It was probably after the death and assumption of Mary that
the so-called 'Gospel of the Infancy' (i.e., the first two chapters
of St Matthew and St Luke) were given their present place at the
beginning of these two Gospels. This Gospel of the Infancy
represents a departure from the usual plan of instructional narrative which always begins with the preaching of John the Baptist. It is a collection of memories, and the source, at least of Luke's

first two chapters, is discreetly left to the imagination. 'And Mary kept all these things, pondering them in her heart' (Luke ii, 19, 51).

About that time John, the only surviving one of the apostles who had followed Christ until his death, produced the book of Revelation, his 'spiritual gospel'. He had meditated for years in the light of the Holy Spirit, and the episodes he relates have a purpose over and above that of completing what the other evangelists had left unsaid. They are chosen for their depth of meaning; everything is calculated, not only the order in which they are written but the least words and even the silences, to show that 'Jesus is the Christ, the Son of God' (John xx, 19).

In the book of Revelation the author definitely alludes to the Virgin Mary when he speaks of 'a woman clothed with the sun, with the moon under her feet, and on her head a crown of twelve stars' (Rev. xii, 1). The Fourth Gospel tells of two important events related one with the other—the presence of Mary at the marriage feast of Cana, and her presence on Calvary.

If we regroup these all too brief observations into a synthesis, we discover that within the New Testament itself a real development of the body of revelation relating to Mary may be traced. 'It is by the apostolic writings that we can best follow this progressive and homogeneous development over some fifty years. In them we find witness of the growing faith of the early Church in regard to Mary. These words—the words of the Holy Spirit himself—trace the line of the Church's development in thought and practice, and confirm the Church's belief that the vocation of Mary lies at the very core of the economy of salvation. This belief has its great Catholic affirmation in Mariology. Hence, in order to judge every manifestation of devotion to Mary wisely we must bear in mind this economy of salvation by Christ.'[1]

1. Michalon, 'Le témoignage du N.T. sur la Mère de Jésus', *Lumière et Vie* No. 10, (1953), p. 125.

IV. MARY IN THE MIDST OF US

We must, however, recognize how restrained the New Testament is on the subject of Mary. This relative effacement is surely the mark of an intention on the part of the Holy Spirit. It invites our attention. Where a detail has been preserved for us, it is because it is of major importance to us, and because the Holy Spirit desires us to stop and reflect on it. Mary knew how to pass unnoticed by her fellow-beings just as Jesus himself did during his hidden life. The only thing said of Jesus during these years was that he was 'the son of the carpenter'. It was his only point of reference, his only status in Nazareth. Outside the village this origin was a very mediocre title to nobility. 'Can anything good come out of Nazareth?' (John i, 46). The people of the village used to say: 'Is not his mother called Mary?' (Matt. xiii, 55).

It is still more unreasonable to be surprised at the Gospels' reticence about Mary in view of the fact that she would naturally have been a very spiritual and silent person. When the angel speaks to her she takes her time to reflect on the meaning of his words. Twice the Gospel says that she kept in her heart the events of which she was witness.

Besides, nothing is more difficult to describe than a spiritual life, for the action of God in a soul is mysterious and cannot be expressed in human words. And the nearer a soul is to God, the more simple is its prayer and the more it baffles description. Could anything be more simple, in fact, than the words: 'I am the handmaid of the Lord', but what could be more untranslatable, more difficult to comment upon? It is not necessary to invent, to give free range to a fertile imagination and attribute to Mary words she never said and sentiments she never expressed. It is not necessary to indulge in enervating sentimentality which would distort the image of that simple, silent and strong character. True, the Gospel is restrained about Mary, but this restraint has a great eloquence for one who knows how to take it and listen to it.

St Thérèse of the Child Jesus, with her strong and practical intelligence and her intuition sharpened by genuine spirituality, sensed this deeply. She would have liked to show 'to what degree the life of the Blessed Virgin is little known'. 'It should not be necessary to say improbable things about her which are not known, for example, that as a very small girl she went to the Temple to offer herself to God, filled with burning sentiments of love and an extraordinary fervour, since she probably went there (if she did this) simply in obedience to her parents.[1] If a sermon on the Blessed Virgin is to bear fruit, her real life as we glimpse it in the Gospels, and not a fictionalized life, should be shown. And one can well imagine that her real life, at Nazareth and later, must have been an ordinary one. "And he was subject to them." How simple it is! The Blessed Virgin is always portrayed as unapproachable. She should be portrayed as someone possible to imitate, practising the hidden virtues, that is to say, *living her faith as we live ours,* and this should be proved from the Bible, where we read: "And they did not understand the saying which he spoke to them" (Luke ii, 50).'[2]

We must try to forget Mary as represented and sometimes caricatured by certain forms of art and piety over the past twenty centuries, and see her as she really was and lived: the young Jewish girl, then the young woman of the people, with nothing to distinguish her from others, speaking the language of the country with the accent of her native Galilee.

Let us not imagine that because she was immaculate from her conception and was to become the Mother of God, Mary did not have to live her faith as we do, to go to God as we go, experiencing the same difficulty in prayer, accepting the sorrows and sufferings of life and making the same efforts we should make to discover the hand of God in them.

Some people think that Mary had the grace of advance en-

1. And she probably did not go there at all.
2. *Novissima verba,* Sayings of St Thérèse of Lisieux (London, 1929).

lightenment about all the events of her life, whose profound meaning was supernaturally revealed to her. What is the use of such strange ideas, which the Gospels in any case contradict? Had God excluded from Mary's life the dimness of faith together with the total abandonment into the hands of God which it demands, then she would not have been one of us, not our model. Happily for us, however, Mary is truly one of our race, for she knew by experience what it was to believe without seeing and without understanding.

At first glance we might imagine that the apparition of the angel was so decisive that Mary was spared any effort of faith. We could also imagine that the family life of continual intimacy with Jesus was for Mary a life of almost heavenly contemplation, where direct vision rendered all faith superfluous.

We shall see that it was nothing of the sort. Obviously the visit of an angel can give a momentary shock. But Gabriel's words were very mysterious and the interview only lasted a few moments. After that it was a matter of living long years and waiting patiently. As for her life with Jesus, it probably perplexed rather than helped her faith. Was not that the experience of the apostles?

Mary was a human being of flesh and blood like ourselves. She was not preserved either from suffering or from spiritual aridity. She was simply preserved from sin, and from the apathy and lack of perception which result from original sin. Since Mary was immaculate, she was all the more capable of living continually in faith.

Mary was not a disembodied spirit. She was the betrothed and subsequently the wife of Joseph. As though to dispense Mary from knowing a truly human love, he has been represented as a greybeard of advanced years. But why should she not have loved Joseph with her woman's heart, since all love comes from God himself? (1 John iv, 7). She was the mother of a little child who grew up and became a man, thanks to a very human and very genuine mother's love.

She belonged to a much more clearly defined and compact social milieu than the ones we know, which influence individuals so forcibly. She knew all the problems that belonged to her station and state in life, and her experience was sufficiently wide to light up the way of ordinary humans like ourselves.

Christians today can recognise themselves in the religious attitudes of Mary. Like all wives and mothers she experienced both joy and suffering, and the life she lived was the very ordinary, very dull life of women of humble station. But the Gospel shows us that Mary's attitude was spontaneously religious in all the events of that life. Her faith, her sense of God, her humility, her charity, her unselfishness and her discretion show through the most insignificant facts of her life and are qualities which she really possessed.

V. DID MARY GROW IN FAITH?

Those immensely meaningful words which Elizabeth spoke to Mary at the visitation: 'And *blessed is she who believed* that there would be a fulfilment of what was spoken to her from the Lord' (Luke i, 45) seem to sum up her whole life and character.

Mary had staked her life on the word of God. But Elizabeth knew what faith was, and also had just experienced in her own home, in the person of her husband who was struck dumb, what lack of faith was. Elizabeth's praise of Mary defines her whole spiritual character. She is the one who believed. In the case of such a faith, can we admit to a growth, a life-long education by the Holy Spirit?

Let us examine three reasons why we can answer in the affirmative. In the first place, all the divine calls in the Bible are vocations of continual growth. This is true of the chosen people, and it is true also of individuals. Everything is said at the first calling, yet everything has to be discovered by degrees, as in a process of slow maturing. We have only to think of Abraham,

Jeremiah or Paul. In Paul's case, his whole future teaching is epitomized in the lightning dialogue on the road to Damascus. Nevertheless, if we read the epistles of St Paul in chronological order we find ourselves watching the development of a mind becoming progressively aware of itself and gradually recording and setting in order the riches of the first insight. The word 'maturing' is accurate up to a certain point, but the word 'education' is the right one, because it is God who directs this growth by his Holy Spirit. He says everything when sowing the first seed, but he makes the seed grow in the heart of the person whom he has called, using the events of his or her life to do so.

The second reason is of a psychological order. In all knowledge there are two stages: the stage of notional acquisition, and what we would venture to call the stage of existential knowledge. There are many things, particularly in the sphere of faith, which we have always known with our minds, but which, one day, we suddenly 'realize' with our whole being. This second stage is never final; it gives rise, in its turn, to successive discoveries the last of which we are well aware is yet to come, and the most brilliant of which is darkness itself compared with the vision to which we know ourselves called. Mary cannot have been exempt from these psychological laws and, at the time the Evangelist was writing the story of the infancy of Jesus, she certainly had a more penetrating insight into the words she had heard and the things she had experienced than on the first day.

The third reason is that the Gospel episodes touching on our Lady are not so dissimilar as they appear to be. She is in fact often shown in identical situations, and the words Jesus addresses to her are in the same tone, whatever the circumstances or whoever the Evangelist reporting the episode. The 'Why do you search for me?' reported by Luke in his account on the finding in the Temple, the 'Woman, what have you to do with me?' reported by John in his account of the marriage feast of Cana, and the 'Who are my mother and my brothers?' reported by Mark, all proceed from the same steadfast educational intention on the part of Jesus. He wishes to form the faith of his mother by calling on her to surpass herself, to leave the plane of a simple human love in order to rise to that of a love inspired by God, so that she may become capable of embracing a multitude of children.

It is necessary to abandon the static idea of vocation in the case of Mary just as in our own case. Even our vocabulary bears the trace of this erroneous conception: we always speak of a vocation in the past tense, we have 'received' such or such a vocation, and want to be left in peace once and for all. We have heard a call and responded, and that is that. We feel inclined to ask, like Peter: 'What then shall we have?' But it is now that we are being called, and today's call is more urgent than yesterday's. God's plan for us is greater than the one we thought we had discovered, and the thing is that we should keep moving forward.

Mary's vocation developed and grew in her with the passing of the years and the events she experienced, which we are now about to describe. She heard God's call in all its reality on the day of the annunciation and she responded to it with a total faith. The Holy Spirit caused this faith to grow throughout her whole life.

VI. ABRAHAM AND MARY

There seems little in common between Abraham and Mary; between the founder of the Jewish race and his distant descendant; between the great nomad and the young girl of Israel.

Nevertheless, anyone who tries to go beyond the superficial texture of events in order to grasp their spiritual significance will find many points of resemblance.

The characterization of the two is equally stylized. We have already compared Abraham with David to see in what detail the Bible has presented us with David's portrait in bold relief, while Abraham's has been greatly simplified: we cannot form a mental picture of Abraham's features, either physical or moral; he is only a response to a call, a 'Yes' given to God. The same is true of Mary. Compare her portrait in the Bible with St Peter's: his character is very sharply drawn, his words and actions reveal him clearly. Of Mary's temperament we can say nothing: her picture shows absolute simplicity, and that is all we can say of her, even when we add up all we have been told and shown of her.

It is the very simplicity of their biblical image that enables both Abraham and Mary to generate endless reflection. The history of Abraham and the witness of his faith were the subject of a theological development which came to its full flowing in the epistle to the Romans and the epistle to the Hebrews. Similarly, the faith of our Lady has been, for the last two thousand years, the subject of the Church's reflection and of a valid theological development, under the guidance of the Holy Spirit.

Just as Abraham contained in himself all the people of Israel, so Mary contained in herself the Church, the new people of Israel, of which she is the mother.

This general impression is confirmed when we examine the history of Abraham and of Mary step by step. God intervenes personally and paternally in the life of both. His call is at the same time a promise. Each is promised not only a miraculous son, but also an immense spiritual posterity. These promises, which are separated by an interval of twenty centuries, are supported by the same solemn affirmation that with God nothing is impossible.

Abraham and Mary both respond with their faith. Abraham comes to know the living God, and his experience so influences his descendants down the centuries that Mary at once accepts the fact that this living God, the Lord, will do wonders in her.

Their hope is absolute. Abraham, who is ninety-nine years old and is promised a son by God, has a counterpart in Mary to whom God makes a similar promise although she is a virgin. Abraham's response, 'Here am I' (Gen. xxii, 11), to God's demand that he sacrifice Isaac, prepares the way for Mary's response: 'Behold, I am the handmaid of the Lord' (Luke i, 38).

Mary's faithfulness, too, is like Abraham's when she is faced with the same trials. The same initial renunciation is imposed on both. Impossible and painful situations follow for the one and the other. Each is asked to sacrifice an only son, and Mary has to bear the pain of seeing her sacrifice completed.

Abraham is the father of those who believe, while Mary is their mother. 'And blessed is she who believed' (Luke i, 45). Mary's faith is the goal, the summit of the faith of the people of Israel, which is rooted in the faith of Abraham. It is at the same time the starting-point of the faith of the Church. Abraham's faith rested upon the omnipotence of the living God; Mary's rested at the same time on the one to come. And the faith of the Church in the divinity of Jesus Christ first came to life in the soul of Mary.

9.

From the One God to the Holy Trinity

I. THE KNOWLEDGE OF THE ONE GOD

1. *The God of the Old Testament*. We know from Mary's reply to the angel and from her Magnificat what a very keen sense of the living God she had. We know the names she gives him, names which show the adoration, respect, and obedience of her whole being. She calls him the Lord, the Almighty. She declares herself his handmaid. She sees him clearly at work in her and in the world. In this she is the heir of all the religious education that God has given his people since Abraham. God has intervened so often to challenge or guide Israel that the faithful Jews whom we hear speaking at the dawn of the New Testament—Simeon, Anna, Elizabeth, Zechariah, Mary—give a very personal tone to their prayer.

Thus Mary is led by the Bible itself to a deeply religious awareness of the closeness and majesty of the living God.

2. *It is then that the angel comes to announce God's message to her*. Of course, Mary does not immediately see the full import of the angel's words, so enveloped in mystery, which leave her completely free to take the step which her faith dictates. It is through her faith that she finds herself before the face of God, and she simply says that she is the handmaid of the Lord. In a sense this is her true name, for in the few words spoken by her in the Gospel stories she twice calls herself the handmaid of the Lord. For her, God really is the Almighty. Because she is humble and lowly before him, she is fit to become his instrument.

She remains for ever the handmaid of the Lord, side by side with him whom the prophets called the 'Servant of God'. After the Last Supper and just before his passion Jesus could repeat with profound truth those words of the Hallel: 'I am thy servant, the son of thy handmaid' (Ps. cxvi, 16).

In her short meeting Mary receives great inspiration, dazzling yet at the same time obscure, like everything that comes from God and demands the faith of his creature. She does not reason and argue like Eve. She does not say: 'I will do my best', but simply 'Be it done unto me'. This is the Christian attitude in its first abounding expression. Mary, faced with the call of God, does not even think of herself or look into herself. Everything is quite simple for her because her soul truly belongs to God. What is simpler than to say 'Yes' to God, to consent to being guided by him, and never to go back on this consent?

3. Some time later, during her visit to Elizabeth, *she addresses her canticle, the Magnificat, to God.*

The first impression of this canticle is that it is a mosaic of quotations from the Old Testament.[1] It seems to lack originality. It is impersonal; its literary genre is well known and makes it akin not only to the canticles of the Old Testament but also to those of the New, such as Zechariah's Benedictus. But if we examine it closely we find that it throws much light on Mary's mind and on the direction of her meditation and prayer. Mary had been brought up on the Old Testament, which she knew almost by heart like the Jews of her time, and when she expressed herself in prayer she spontaneously used the biblical forms of prayer. It was the same with our Lord's prayer.

Her prayer is centred on God, not on herself; it is full of thanksgiving and praise.

Nevertheless one objection springs to mind. Can we be sure that this is not a prayer composed *post eventum* by the evangelist, like the invented speeches that Livy the Roman historian put into the mouths of his characters? How could Mary remember so

1. See the canticle of Hannah, the mother of Samuel (1 Sam. ii, 1-10; cf. Ps. cxiii, 7-9).

long afterwards the words she had spoken in a moment of great spiritual exaltation? Sixty or seventy years had certainly elapsed between the time she first uttered the Magnificat and the time it was written down.

The discourse was certainly written down long after the event, but the Magnificat contains so much that was intrinsic to her deepest thoughts and feelings that Mary obviously never had to make any effort to think, feel and pray in this way. In his book on our Lady, Jean Guitton writes: 'She could say of her Magnificat what Corot said of a painting he had done very quickly, when he was asked how long it had taken: "Five minutes—and all my life."' Besides, Mary did not have to remember the exact words of her prayer in order to give them to St Luke. The content is what matters, the profound and permanent substance of the prayer. The words may be forgotten and then recalled differently, but the substance remains the same.

4. The Magnificat consists of two parts—the story of Mary in God, and the story of God in the world.

(a) *The Story of Mary in God* (Luke i, 46-49).

We can see now that the Magnificat is not as impersonal as it appeared at first sight. Side by side with the quotations from the Old Testament, there are sentences which can only have come from Mary and which only apply to her.

'For he who is mighty has done great things for me.' God does great things always, but what he has done today is even greater, and he has done it for Mary. God fulfils his promises and he fulfils the hope of the prophets, but it is for Mary that he does this in his plan to do great things in her. And it is in doing these things that he remembers his love and the promise made to Abraham. Mary therefore sees herself at the centre of God's plan and work for the world.

'For behold, henceforth all generations will call me blessed.' This is not only the reparation of the curse that had once fallen on Eve, and the restoration, in Mary, of women's dignity, but also the basis of the Church's cult of Mary. And one simple expression evokes all her spiritual posterity, all her sons and daughters who are the counterpart of Abraham's spiritual posterity. Thus Mary is the origin and the mother of all redeemed generations.

'For he has regarded the low estate of his handmaiden.' God has formed his people by trials, and has thus given the best souls among them the possibility of great hope and an awareness of the need for his grace. Mary is the mouthpiece of these poor people who yearn and listen for God.

(b) *The Story of God in the world* (Luke i, 50–55).

Mary sees God at work in the world, guiding the course of events with his mighty hand, ordering them mercifully from generation to generation, in sovereign command of everything that man does. What a sound philosophy of history! In the eyes of Mary, who knows the living God, the hand of the Almighty holds, controls and permits everything that happens. God has his plan and he realizes it when it pleases him, by the play of events, even if men appear to be in control. Faith consists in seeing the hand of God in everything, for the most lowly or disconcerting events only occur with his permission, and they are the very means by which he expresses his love.

II. MARY LEARNS TO KNOW THE SON OF GOD

While the knowledge of the one God is the starting-point of Mary's faith, it is also destined to increase during her whole life. *Mary is to be the first of God's creatures to receive the revelation of the Holy Trinity*, not, of course, in a dogmatic or conceptual form but in the course of a living experience.

Mary is to be initiated into the mystery of the Trinity through her Son. How did Mary come to know the Son of God, who had become her own son? Can we describe the path of this knowledge from what the Gospel tells us? To speak of a path will seem rather bold when we recall the story of the annunciation. Twice the angel announces that he who is to be born is the Son of God; but what use are words, even those most pregnant with meaning, if we do not give them time to mature in the heart? Mary must definitely have been struck by the words of the angel, which echoed well-known prophecies. Even those striking words: 'The power of the Most High will overshadow you', must have made her guess that God was going to enter into her as he had once entered the ark of the covenant. But would this presence be permanent? 'The message did not contain any clear indication that our Lady was to consider the presence of her son in her womb as equivalent to God's presence in the Temple.'[1]

Mary certainly had a basic understanding from the outset, but she had to go on gaining deeper knowledge. We have an indication of this in the incident of the finding of Jesus in the Temple, where we see that Mary does not understand the child's reply. It must have been all very mysterious, and the manifestation of the Messiah seemed to be delayed indefinitely. Obviously, Mary was well aware whose son Jesus was, but this faith was daily tried by waiting. And yet she kept all these things in her heart, and waited for God's own time.

This is why the knowledge of her son's divinity remained a mystery for so long. During the nine months of her pregnancy she was the dwelling-place of the Word Incarnate and hence the first mortal to encounter this mystery of faith. At Bethlehem it was a little baby that Mary carried in her arms. How difficult it must have been for her to see Jesus except as a baby just like any other while she watched him grow up to be like any other man; for the growth of a human being is a desperately slow business. Living with Jesus cannot have made faith easier. It must, on the contrary, have exercised it, tried it and often challenged it.

Mary had to become used to tending her child, who allowed himself to be looked after and did not look in the least more

1. Galot, *Marie dans l'Evangile*, p. 60.

inspired than any of the neighbouring women's babies. She had to become used to teaching him the simple words of the local dialect, those words which all mothers teach their little ones and of which the first are 'papa' and 'mamma'. Then she had to tell him what to do as all mothers tell their little boys. Of course there was no question of her having to correct bad tendencies in this perfect child. But she had to accustom him to daily life, adapt him to the social milieu, and initiate him progressively into the customs of the country and the conditions of life in the village community. It must have been very easy for Mary to manage this child, because when giving her memories to the evangelist Luke in her old age, she remembered his obedience with tenderness, and recalled her astonishment at the only act of independence in his childhood, on his first visit to Jerusalem.

For Mary in particular this episode must have been a psychological shock and no doubt marked the beginning of a new stage in her knowledge of the divinity of Jesus. Until then Jesus had been known to everyone as the son of Joseph. When Mary spoke of Joseph to him no doubt she called him 'your father', and these habits had a deep psychological effect on her. She speaks to Jesus of 'your father and I', and he at once replies with 'my Father's house'. The reply must have been painful to Mary, not only because of the tone but also because of the divine mystery of his short answer. She does not understand the meaning of Jesus' words, but are we straining the texts if we surmise that in Mary's memory and reflections the reply of Jesus was the next important event after the words of the angel Gabriel? From the time of the annunciation and its glorious but profoundly mysterious message, Mary's thoughts on the subject could quite legitimately have lain dormant. For what could be less mysterious than a child growing up day after day? But the words spoken by Jesus in Jerusalem are no longer the words of a child. It is clear that immediately afterwards he returned to his normal submissiveness and the daily routine of family life. But once spoken, these words are irrevocable and unforgettable and they leave behind them the trail of faith.

For over twenty years more Mary is witness to something as misleading as it could possibly be. The son who had been announced in such a magnificent way and whose miraculous origin she is well aware of, works as a carpenter, nothing he says or does is in the least remarkable, and he passes quite unnoticed among his fellows.

And now Jesus goes away from home in circumstances which are unknown to us, leaving his mother wondering over those other mysterious words, spoken at the marriage feast at Cana, which she probably understood no better than the earlier ones—and do we ourselves understand them any better now, after twenty centuries of reflection? But failure to understand fully is not the same as failure to believe, and faith certainly admits of what may be called an initial, incomplete understanding. This starting-point is enough to give a first impetus to faith which is, above all else, an adherence of one person to another. Henceforthward Mary lives united in mind and heart to Jesus but without his physical presence, and this is a new stage in her faith. She follows at a distance this son who is entirely taken up with the work of his heavenly Father.

No doubt she hears of the miracles he performs, but it is unlikely that she sees them with her own eyes since in Nazareth, where she normally lives, Jesus can work no miracles, for 'a prophet is not without honour, except in his own country' (Mark vi, 4-5). We would like to be able to compare the growth of the apostles' faith in Jesus, the Son of God, with Mary's faith in the divinity of her son. Mary *knew* of his divinity from the day of the annunciation. This seed of faith had been growing slowly during the years at Nazareth, especially in moments of great trial like the prophecy of Simeon and the three days' anxiety in Jerusalem, under the shock of suffering and the pondering of mysterious words. It was to expand rapidly during the public ministry of her son. The miracle at Cana, for instance, where according to St John the disciples first saw the glory of Jesus, had far more significance for Mary than for them because it put the angel Gabriel's message in a new light.

Once more a trial—and what a trial—came to put everything in question again, or rather to give it a new basis. Did Mary clearly know that her son's ministry would lead to his death? And when she saw him dead, did she know for certain that he would rise again? Here again we must accept the laws of normal psychology. Mary may very well have known the prophecies which Jesus was later to explain to his disciples on the way to Emmaus. And yet we must admit that for a normal mind—and Mary's was like our own—the loss of a life, and especially the defeat of Calvary, could not be a sign of power. Similarly, the sight of a corpse—more especially that of an only son—was so bound up in Mary's mind with the finality of death that her faith in the resurrection must have been overshadowed by the intense suffering of her bereavement.

Let us make what we mean clearer. The faith of the twelve was to founder in the drama of the passion, but the faith of Mary could not break down at this stage of its progress in the same way. The place given her in St John's Gospel shows that Mary, on the contrary, had entered into the meaning of the Easter mystery. But this faith continues in the midst of normal psychological reactions and a mother's love overwhelmed by the suffering and death of an only son.

It must also be stressed that during the whole of our Lord's earthly life Mary's faith was enriched by his physical presence in her own world. Let us compare her faith with ours. We do, of course, believe in Christ, but this Christ, the Son of God, whom we never reach except in the invisible world, dwells in a light so inaccessible that we would almost do without the human body which the Word of God has willed to take for us to touch with our hands in the sacraments; and we would almost be content with the divinity of Christ alone. Without giving the word its full technical sense, let us recognize that we all tend to be Mono-physites. And let us remember how strongly St Teresa of Avila insisted on the necessity of our never forgetting the sacred humanity of our Lord in our Christian life.[1] Mary did not experience this danger, because her habitual world was so filled with the physical presence of Jesus. And we should always enrich our own faith with her experience.

The faith of Mary in the divine sonship of Jesus had to reach a new and final stage: in our Lord's resurrection and ascension. For her, as for the apostles, it was good that Jesus should go away. We think of the growth of supernatural faith in the same terms as that of some human sentiment. We imagine instinctively that our faith would be greatly helped in its growth by the familiar sight of Christ. But the laws governing the growth of super-natural faith are quite different: it is absence that makes faith increase. 'It is good for you that I go away.' And during the later hidden years of Mary's life she was still with her son by faith, whether she found him in her own heart or saw him in heaven at the right hand of the Father. The promise of Jesus: 'If a man love me, he will keep my word, and my Father will love him, and we will come to him and make our home with him' (John xiv, 23), was realized above all in Mary.

III. THROUGH CHRIST, THE FATHER WAS REVEALED TO HER

As Mary progressed in her faith in the divine sonship of Jesus, she penetrated the mystery of the three distinct persons in God. All her spiritual upbringing in the Old Testament had impressed on her the need to worship God.

She had often heard or said the *shema*: 'Hear Israel, Your God is the only God.' Even the verse of Psalm ii: 'He said to me, "You

1. St Teresa of Avila, *Autobiography*.

are my son, today I have begotten you" ' had prepared Mary's soul for distinguishing the persons of the Trinity, for by her time its interpretation could give some idea of the Messiah's divine origin.

When the angel had announced to her that she would give birth to a son by the intervention of the Holy Spirit and the power of the Most High, she had received the revelation of the Trinity in its essence. But here again we must admit an immense gap between Mary's total adherence to God's word and a profound insight into the depths of the mystery. It took Mary a whole lifetime to cross this gap. She discovered the Father as she grew in the knowledge of the Son who was her own son. This discovery was entirely in line with her Jewish faith. He whom she used to call the Lord, the Almighty, gradually became the Father for her. An important occasion in the history of this growth of Mary's faith was that anxious day in Jerusalem when Jesus replied: 'Did you not know that I must be in my Father's house?' As we know, Mary did not understand the meaning of those words, but she kept them in her heart and allowed them to grow there.

We must add that Mary also discovered the Father by being his handmaid. Mary's obedience is the main and permanent source of her knowledge of the heavenly Father. To serve the Lord God is to know him, to discover him more and more every day. Is not this the meaning of the words of Jesus: 'But he who does what is true comes to the light' (John iii, 21)? To do what is true—does not this mean obeying the Father and therefore coming to know him more and more? We must admit that Mary was the first to experience in advance the force of these words which Jesus spoke later. This does not necessarily imply that Jesus gave his mother special instructions before his public ministry. But the example of Jesus during his hidden life, and more especially during his adult years at Nazareth, must have been a deep and lasting source of inspiration for Mary. Even before he began to preach, the will of his heavenly Father was the daily food of Jesus. And before his mother's eyes he lived in the spirit of his later words: 'But I do as the Father has commanded me, so that the world may know that I love the Father' (John xiv, 31).

IV. MARY KNEW THE HOLY SPIRIT BY BEING EDUCATED BY HIM

It is more difficult when we come to speak of Mary's knowledge of the Holy Spirit. The Holy Spirit, we might say, has no countenance. The Bible speaks of the face of God, and in the Gospels the voice of the Father is heard several times. And Christ has a body, a voice and a face familiar to Mary. But the Holy Spirit only makes his presence felt by what he does, in the mysterious form of a dove, or the still more mysterious form of a tongue of fire.

But Mary had the unique experience of her union with the Holy Spirit on the day of the annunciation. She could never forget that intimate union when, by her *fiat*, she became the miraculous spouse of the Father and agreed to co-operate with the Holy Spirit in giving human birth to Jesus the Messiah. A woman does not forget the intimacy of a great love. And Mary experienced the intimacy of 'the everlasting Love' that day.

And let us not forget that Mary was present at Pentecost! The Holy Spirit is faithful in his love.

She was the first Christian to be educated by the presence of the Holy Spirit who had entered into her. We all know from St Paul that the Holy Spirit is the author of our faith, and the apostle even says that: 'No one can say "Jesus is Lord" except by the Holy Spirit' (1 Cor. xii, 3).

It is also the Holy Spirit who inspires our prayer. St Paul tells us that here the Holy Spirit comes to the aid of our weakness: 'For we do not know how to pray as we ought, but the Spirit himself intercedes for us with sighs too deep for words' (Rom. viii, 26).

Mary received the Holy Spirit at the annunciation. She

received him, not as a fleeting visitant, but as the permanent presence of him who is the source of faith, the power of prayer, and the inspiration of love. Mary knew the Holy Spirit in faith by allowing herself to be guided by him.

10

The Growth of Mary's Hope

I. THE ANNUNCIATION

FROM the day of the annunciation God demands Mary's total obedience. But he supports this call by a sign which is very clear to her. For the Angel says to Mary: 'And behold, your kinswoman Elizabeth in her old age has also conceived a son; and this is the sixth month with her who was called barren. For with God nothing will be impossible' (Luke i, 36–37). Most of the children of destiny in the Bible—Jacob, Joseph, Samson, Samuel, and finally John the Baptist—were born in exceptional circumstances. That is to say, they were born of mothers long barren. Our Lady, the mother of the Messiah, comes at the end of this long tradition. She is 'the greater counterpart of those other barren women—Sarah, Rebekah, Rachel, Hannah, Elizabeth—'[1] who bear children. The angel's allusion is all the more clear since he quotes the words already used to confirm the faith of Sarah: 'For with God nothing will be impossible' (Gen. xviii, 14). All the Old Testament miraculous births (where barrenness is cured) are of messianic personages, whether *ancestors* of the Messiah (cf. the genealogy of Jesus according to St Matthew) or messianic *figures* (Samson, for instance). The angel presents the favour granted to Elizabeth not only as a repetition of the miraculous births of the past but also as the foreshadowing of the supernatural conception of Jesus. From that time the words of the angel enter into Mary's heart and memory. She will recall them every time some event comes to try her.

Mary's reply: 'I am the handmaid of the Lord', reveals her

1. R. P. Bernard, *L'Annonciation de Marie, l'Eglise.*

profound obedience, her total abandonment to God. This obedience inspired by faith renders the redemption possible. As Pope St Leo was later to say: *Prius concepit mente quam corpore*—'She conceived by her faith before conceiving in her body.' Thus, the redemption of all mankind begins with this 'Yes'. Mary is for ever bound by this 'Yes' which commits her to her destiny, and in her person the Church accepts God's plan of salvation and collaborates in it.

II. MARY'S SILENCE TOWARDS JOSEPH

It would seem as though Mary had said everything perfectly in accepting God's plan and that there was no further place in her soul for an increase of hope. But we must consider the laws of psychology and the long time required for all spiritual development. And this is why God tries Mary's hope by asking her consent and then placing her in impossible situations where she is asked to give herself completely to God.

It is in this spirit that we should read the little episode told by St Matthew (i, 18-25), an episode that we would prefer to pass over in silence because it is somewhat embarrassing. Mary has just received an announcement which upsets her life. She says nothing about it to her betrothed but goes away for three months to the home of her cousin Elizabeth. When she returns to Nazareth she still remains silent about it. Her condition becomes visible. Joseph, no doubt hoping to avoid scandal, decides to break off his engagement, though his confidence in Mary remains unshaken. Were it not for his absolute confidence in her, he would, as a just man strictly faithful to the Law, be obliged to have her stoned to death. But because of his astounding confidence in Mary, Joseph bows before the mystery, and by doing so becomes the most indisputable witness to the fact that the child has truly been conceived by God alone.

What does Mary's silence towards Joseph mean, especially

when compared with the joy and even exuberance of the visitation? Mary takes a long and hurried journey to help Elizabeth. But she does not say a word or even give a hint to Joseph, who lives in the same village. Why does she remain silent when it would be so simple and so normal to speak, especially to such an upright, just and devout man as Joseph? Why this silence, since she knows very well that it will worry Joseph?

We find the first explanation in the content of the angel's message. The angel had mentioned Elizabeth as an example of miraculous motherhood. Elizabeth too had received a divine revelation, and this revelation, similar to Mary's, united their destinies in one joint plan. This was enough for Mary to share her joy without being in any way indiscreet.

On the other hand, the angel had not said a word about Joseph. Mary was engaged to Joseph, a descendant of David, but the angel had given her no indication about their intended marriage. Was this arrangement to stand, or was it imperilled? God alone could speak, as and when it pleased him. Had he not taken over the whole initiative in Mary's life? He had sent her his message, and done all things in her. It was for him, then, to tell Joseph if he was to have a place in the unfolding of his plan. It was not for Mary to speak. On the contrary, she was to remain absolutely silent, because the message and the gift of God are his divine prerogative, of which no one may presume to speak. It was not possible to encroach on the divine will, because the omnipotence and autonomy of God must be respected.

But what would happen if Mary remained silent? What would Joseph think, and what would he do? In order to keep calm and silent Mary had only to recall the words of the Angel: 'For with God nothing will be impossible.'

Joseph was certainly thoughtful and worried. We know that he was even thinking of breaking off his engagement. We do not know Mary's thoughts, but we can imagine how worried she was about the future, about possible scandal, and about the suffering of losing Joseph's respect and her own reputation, as well as the pain of causing Joseph to suffer when a single word could clear up everything. For a sensitive person, is there any suffering worse than knowing that one is the cause of another's suffering?

It was God who willed this silent drama. What proves this express will of God is the fact that the angel could have been sent much sooner. But God waited until the inner development of the crisis had reached its climax in Joseph's decision to break with Mary, and sent the angel only to stop the decision being put into effect. This shows a desire to train the faith of Mary and Joseph by suffering.

Both were to have many painful experiences, but they all sprang from God's wish to educate them. No one could yet know the painful road which the Son of God Incarnate would have to travel to save the world, but Joseph and Mary learn from the first, by experience rather than sudden insight, that it is not possible to be associated with the work of Christ without treading the path of sacrifice.

III. THE PROPHECY OF SIMEON

In this episode, so full of meaning, we can see what it was that tried Mary's hope. Simeon, after extolling the mission of the Messiah who was to be 'a light for revelation to the Gentiles', and causing Mary and Joseph to 'marvel at what was said about the child', simply turned to Mary and said to her without more ado: 'Behold, this child is set for the fall and rising of many in Israel, and for a sign that is spoken against' (Luke ii, 34). Needless to say this prophecy was a great trial for Mary, and the contradiction between the words of the old man and the angel Gabriel's announcement of the child's future glory must have been a real puzzle to her. How, in fact, could the prophecy of the throne of David be reconciled with that of the sign to be contradicted? She certainly knew the prophecy of Isaiah about the suffering servant

nd also all the prophecies about the glorious Messiah. Simeon's
words confirm Mary in her certainty that Jesus is the Messiah,
ut the words emphasizing her future sorrows pierce her heart
nd yet give her hope.

V. THE FLIGHT INTO EGYPT AND THE MASSACRE OF THE INNOCENTS

We must look realistically at the material conditions of this
xile: the poverty of refugees, their insecurity as immigrants
vithout means of support. Mary must be asking searching
questions. Why is God acting as he is with the child and herself?
What is God's design which is being worked out through these
pparently disconnected events? Where are the throne of David
nd the everlasting kingdom announced by the angel? True,
Simeon's prophecy of the sword of sorrow was becoming
learer, but all the rest was becoming so much more obscure.

And then there was the massacre of the little children which
Mary must have heard about either during the flight—for news
ravels faster than people—or on their return to Palestine. Why
ad God permitted the bloody sacrifice of these young lives
which he had allowed to come into being? Why had the angel,
ent to warn Joseph at night on God's instructions, not also
warned the other parents of the danger threatening their children?
Why does God give mothers cause to weep? Where does the
goodness of God come in? The Gospel definitely tells us nothing
f Mary's thoughts, but the facts are there, and it is good to think
hat Mary was confronted with the same insoluble problems as
we are, and that her hope too was put to the test. She learned, in
order that we may learn it from her, that it is in the obscurity of
aith that one must resolutely affirm that God is as kind as a father
o his children.

V. THE HIDDEN LIFE

Mary must have renewed her hope constantly during the long

years of the hidden life in Nazareth, so devoid of apparen
importance. Otherwise she could not have avoided an occasiona
fleeting thought that she might perhaps have misunderstood the
Angel's words and that this village carpenter, so like all the othe
Jews of Nazareth, was not, after all, the Son of God.

Hope is a virtue which is renewed every day. It cannot grow
except by asserting itself in face of impossible situations. Mary
lived it in her life until the day when Jesus, dying on the cross
seemed to be definitely deprived of the throne of David. She
knew how to hope without ever seeing the promises made to he
realized. Abraham and his first descendants had to persevere in
hope in just the same way. 'These all died in faith, not having
received what was promised, but having seen it and greeted i
from afar, and having acknowledged that they were strangers and
exiles on the earth' (Heb. xi, 13).

II.

Mary is Educated in Faithfulness by God

FAITHFULNESS is almost synonymous with love. When God made a covenant with his people he demanded that faithfulness should be Israel's response to his faithfulness. God is often called faithful, and this faithfulness is an essential attribute of his. It is because he loves, and loves eternally, that 'his faithfulness spreads to those who fear him from generation to generation'.

When God calls, he appeals to love, and every vocation is an invitation to love God with all our heart, with all our mind and with all our strength, and our neighbour as ourselves. But such a love is always developing, because through original sin we are so encumbered by self-love that there is hardly room in our hearts for a true love of God and our neighbour. Until the heart has freed itself from its original selfishness, its fidelity to God has to be ceaselessly tried, formed and strengthened.

But was such an education in faithfulness necessary for Mary, exempt as she was from original sin? Was she not full of grace already, and was not her heart free from all self-love? Of course, we cannot doubt this, but we must admit that Mary was subject to the normal laws of psychology. She had received her vocation. She had accepted it fully as a seed to be cherished. She had yet to discover, stage by stage, the immense range of her vocation and the depth of fidelity that was asked of her. Finally, we must not forget that Mary had been chosen by God as the first soul to be saved by Christ so that her spiritual journey should be an inspiration and an example for us.

God took it in hand to educate Mary in faithfulness, and trials were the means he employed, as we have already seen in the education of Abraham.

I. THE TEST OF TIME AND THE HIDDEN LIFE

Though God had filled Mary with graces he made her submit to the test of time. God always educates souls by the test of time and for this he uses great lengths of years.

The passing of time forces love to grow deeper in order to surmount the monotony of daily life. Mary lived with Jesus for some thirty years. While she had in her memory the glorious and painful prophecies which she had heard, yet she was also faced with this mystery of the Son of God who grew from childhood to adolescence, and in manhood lived and worked as a simple village carpenter—a life without striking incidents, like that of all humble families. The story of the child lost in the Temple barely stands out from the surrounding dimness. Mary could see only a child growing up, a child who obeyed so simply that she could find nothing else to describe those long years than the affirmation of this obedience. There was never a miracle to help her along that road, for we are expressly told that the miracle at Cana was the first that Jesus worked. And yet there were sick people to cure, dead to raise (perhaps Joseph among them), and widows mourning their only sons in Nazareth as elsewhere.

The Gospel tells us nothing else about the hidden life of Mary and Jesus. It must have been a life of great simplicity. Poor people who live by the work of their hands do not write their own history. Mary gave herself to God in the humility of her daily tasks. She kept house for her husband Joseph, then for her son Jesus. This entailed the humble chores of cleaning, baking bread, mending, drawing water from the well, the daily tasks of the housewife of which the Old Testament gives a list: 'She seeks wool and flax and works with willing hands . . . She rises while it is yet night and provides food for her household . . . She puts her hands to the distaff, and her hands hold the spindle. She opens her hand to the poor, and reaches out her hand to the needy . . . She does not eat the bread of idleness' (Prov. xxxi, 13-27).

If we recall that Jesus drew the substance of his parables from his daily experience, can we not perceive throughout his teachings the mark of the long years lived with Mary in Nazareth? 'No one tears a piece from a new garment and puts it upon an old garment; if he does, he will tear the new, and the piece from the new will not match the old' (Luke v, 36). A man normally has little to do with fabrics, clothing or sewing; his knowledge of them generally comes from his womenfolk. 'To what shall I compare the kingdom of God? It is like leaven which a woman took and hid in three measures of meal, till it was all leavened' (Luke xiii, 20-21). There were no bakeries in the time of Jesus and bread-making was one of the essential duties of a woman. When he spoke this parable Jesus seemed to see his mother once more preparing the dough to make bread for the family.

'Or what woman, having ten silver coins, if she loses one coin, does not light a lamp and sweep the house and seek diligently until she finds it? And when she has found it, she calls together her friends and neighbours, saying, "Rejoice with me, for I have found the coin which I had lost" ' (Luke xv, 8-9).

These two passages give us a vivid insight into the life of the Jewish woman of the time, hence of Mary. There was so little money in circulation in those days that ten silver coins were quite a large sum, and the loss of one would be a catastrophe. The houses in Nazareth were very small, consisting of one single room lit only by the door, and to find something that had fallen on the hard-earth floor one had to light a lamp, even in broad daylight. Social bonds are so numerous and close in an eastern village that even the tiniest event, joyful or sorrowful, is shared by friends and neighbours.

Such was the hidden life of the humble Mary. In the Gospel Mary listens to others talking but mostly remains silent herself.

'She has carried in her womb the Son of the Most High . . . She has felt so much by his presence, and there is so much she has to tell about her dear son. But she leaves his praises to everyone else; she hears the shepherds, she does not say a word to the wise men who come to adore her son, and she listens to Simeon and the prophetess Anna. It is only to St Elizabeth that she opens her heart . . . The wonderful things God does to his creatures naturally give rise to silence, rapture and an intense feeling of holiness. And we keep God's secret sealed in unless he himself moves our tongue and urges us to speak.'[1]

II. THE HIDDEN LIFE IN THE HEART OF MARY

Mary lived with Jesus for more than thirty years, but we do not know what Jesus taught her by his words during this long time. The Gospel relates only one single sentence spoken by Jesus to Mary over these years and then it tells us clearly that Mary did not understand his words.

The example of the life of Jesus must have been better than mere words for teaching Mary those Christian paradoxes which make up true wisdom. And seems that this very long and apparently pointless way of life taught her the sense of values shown by her son to Satan at the temptation in the desert, and taught to his disciples in the beatitudes.

Mary had to live face to face with the mystery of God growing as a child, learning to lisp, speaking like a child, and absorbing the knowledge of mankind. When God takes possession of a soul to make it all his own, he makes it dependent on faith. And the closer he desires to draw it to himself, the more completely he deprives it of earthly consolation in order to purify it. God is especially challenging to his friends. Mary never saw Jesus except with the eyes of faith, in the challenging experience of

1. Bossuet, *Elévation sur les mystères.*

their life together. And this had to be so since she was the first Christian woman to be associated with Jesus in his mission.

During the long years of the hidden life of Jesus, it is Mary, and she alone, who is asked to believe that the world will be redeemed by a saviour who carries on a carpenter's trade for which alone he seems to have been born. In this obscure life Mary undertakes to follow God's will, without waiting for proofs, without self-seeking, without giving ear to any of her own disquieting questions. And she will remain firm throughout her life, repeating in the silence of her heart and the dimness of faith: 'I am the hand-maid of the Lord.' The finest thing in a life consecrated to God is not the first action or word whereby that life is dedicated, but the humble daily beginning again that is called perseverance. Mary had faith at a time when no one else had it in the proper sense of the word. It was she who first walked the Church's path of faith.

Jesus lived for more than thirty years under the eyes of Mary. He chose—or rather his heavenly Father chose for him—his family, his environment, and his life as a village carpenter. That is why this long period of life, apparently so useless, is yet so important for us. Humanly speaking, what a loss of time! At eighteen years of age an oriental is mature for his life's work. At the age when Jesus leaves his village, Alexander the Great had conquered the known world, and been several years dead. Jesus is working as a carpenter in a little village. On account of this loss of time, he will only be able to make a fleeting journey through Palestine two or three times. Our Lady was to discover, in her silent meditation, that Jesus was saviour and redeemer from the first moment of his incarnation, and that in his unobtrusive life in Nazareth he was saving the world because he was lovingly obeying his Father's will: 'Consequently, when Christ came into the world . . . he said: "Lo, I have come, to do thy will, O God" ' (Heb. x, 5, 7). It is by seeing Jesus the saviour in Nazareth, doing the will of the heavenly Father, that Mary learned that her own humble daily actions acquired their value from the faith and love that inspired them. St Thérèse of the Child Jesus expresses this experience in these few words: 'He does not need our works but our love.' In this she echoes St John of the Cross: 'In the evening of life, we shall be judged on our love.'

Mary saw the Word of God hide himself, not by isolating himself from men as John the Baptist did, but by mixing with people as much as possible; not by leaving the world but by plunging into it, by disappearing into the anonymity of a village population. And Jesus was to succeed so perfectly in passing unnoticed that, in spite of the fame of his miracles, he was always to be known as the carpenter of Nazareth.

Thus, Mary waited many long years for her son to manifest himself, and when he left Nazareth it was to head for disaster and crucifixion. We do not know when Mary died and was taken up to heaven, but everything goes to show that she died fairly late in life, after the period of the first apostolic preaching.

III. THE DESERT OF THE SOUL AND THE SILENCE OF GOD

It was at once the trial of the desert and of God's silence. True, it was not a desert of sand, but of feelings; a dryness of the soul. Of course she had a son to love, and she loved him tenderly. But what a precarious possession was this child who she knew from the beginning would be a sign that is spoken against. And the silence of God in that bereaved soul was still more trying. Mary had once heard the words of the angel, but if Gabriel had ever visited her again, we would know about it.

During her long life Mary had to live by faith and love without ever again receiving the slightest revelation. She had time to recall and meditate on the divine words with their inexhaustible richness. But these words had been said such a long time ago! And the silence of God is all the more difficult to bear when it follows an extraordinary revelation. The effect of the contrast puts a faithful soul to the test.

IV. THE SLOW DESPOILMENT OF THE HEART

We have said that Mary had a true woman's heart. She experienced genuine, very human love for her husband Joseph. Why would she not have loved Joseph, since the love of God filled a heart that had never been occupied by the selfishness of fallen man? But we have not been told of their life together. We can only presume that Joseph was already dead when the public ministry of Jesus began since the Gospels do not mention him. And in this case we can guess that Mary, like all widows do who mourn a very dear husband, experienced suffering that even the presence of a son cannot remove.

Mary loved her son Jesus with the tenderness and strength of true motherly love; with a tenderness all the greater for her insight into the painful destiny of her child; with all the more strength for knowing his origin and his divine mission. But this mother's love is to be put to the test not once but many times and, paradoxically enough, by Jesus himself. We shall examine later on the aim of this schooling which is to open her human heart more and more to the dimensions of the divine plan, and to the number of children who are to be entrusted to her. We shall confine ourselves here to a brief review of the stages of this challenge.

1. *Jesus is Lost in the Temple: the Three Days in Jerusalem*

This episode of the child lost and found again is important on two counts. First, it stands out sharply in Mary's memory against the sober and monotonous background of the hidden life at Nazareth. For there is every sign of Mary's hand in the evangelist's account of this episode: 'And his mother kept all these things in her heart' (Luke ii, 51). At the time the evangelist was writing about the childhood of Jesus, Mary was advanced in years, and like all old women, only remembered the striking events—the great joys and the great sorrows that have made her grow in faith. Secondly, this episode has a symbolical value. It is a light for Joseph and Mary, for it illumines their future path. They certainly did not understand at the time, but they were to have time to reflect on it and penetrate its meaning.

Mary and Joseph go up to Jerusalem with Jesus. They finish their pilgrimage and set out for home. On noticing that the child is no longer with them, they return to Jerusalem in an agony of anxiety and on the third day find him in the Temple, with the doctors of the Law.

Mary says to the child: 'Son, why have you treated us so? Behold, *your father and I* have been looking for you anxiously.' He replies to them: 'How is it that you sought me? Did you not know that I must be *in my Father's* house?'

These words of Jesus to Mary are very precious because they are the only words that have been preserved for us from the childhood of Jesus. Spoken by Jesus as an adolescent they define his outlook on life: one single thought fills his heart—that of his Heavenly Father. Moreover, in the presence of his foster-father he affirms that he is conscious of his divine sonship, that he knows himself to be the Son of God, and that as such he is at home in the Temple, where it should be quite natural to find him.

This episode is a veritable foreshadowing of the death and resurrection of Jesus. The points of contact between the two events are numerous. Both take place in Jerusalem. The duration of each is three days. The loss of Jesus resembles a death, and the joyful termination of the drama presages the resurrection. Did Jesus perchance wish to prepare his mother for his future Passion and death by making her sense the meaning of Simeon's prophecy about the sword of sorrow?

The evangelist makes it clear that when Jesus asked: 'How is it that you sought me? Did you not know that I must be in my Father's house?', Mary and Joseph did not understand the meaning of his words. This lack of understanding may surprise us at first sight. Twice Mary had been told that the child to be born to her would be the Son of God (Luke i, 32 and 35). How was it that she did not understand the words of Jesus, when they appear so clear to us? Let us not forget that more than thirteen years had elapsed since the annunciation. When Mary spoke about Joseph to Jesus she called him 'your father'. The habit of speaking this way indicates a disposition, a mentality. We see it clearly in Mary's words: 'Behold, your father and I have been looking for you anxiously.' Now, Jesus' reply is really disconcerting. He causes Mary, without any preparation, to leave the human and family plane on which she has lived for some twelve years and move on to the plane of the divine designs. What a violent shock for a woman, for a mother who has not yet recovered from the days of anxiety she has just been through. But for Mary it is an occasion for deepening her faith.

Mary tells him: 'Behold, *your father* and I have been looking for you anxiously.' Jesus replies: 'I must be in *my Father's* house.' He uses the same word that she has used, but changes the possessive pronoun and hence the sense, without warning. It is not surprising that Mary understands the words of the reply as applying to the human and earthly father of whom she was speaking whereas Jesus in his reply refers to the Heavenly Father. This is confusing to the mind, and it is not surprising that Mary did not understand. What should surprise us, on the other hand, is the incomprehensible way in which Jesus addresses his mother. He wishes to form her in faith, to give direction to her outlook; he wishes, in short, as we already said, to prepare her for his Passion.

This whole episode shows Jesus' will to form the heart of Mary, by means of suffering, in a more vigorous faith. Mary suffered deeply during all those anxious hours of searching, when she must often have thought of Simeon's prophecy: 'and a sword will pierce through your own soul'. The stern faith demanded of her is also a suffering for Mary. For it is the act of faith *par excellence*, made in the dark, with a bereaved heart. The evangelist actually says: 'And they did not understand the saying which he spoke to them,' adding immediately: 'And his mother kept all these things in her heart.' 'Mary's mind did not penetrate the meaning of the words, but her soul received them in their full depth as the earth opens itself to a seed and gives it what it needs to grow.'[1]

We must admire the way these few words of Jesus reverberate in Mary's soul. She does not understand them but she treasures and ponders them in her heart. She is fully open to the word of God. Jesus introduces his mother's mind to the mystery of his mission as Redeemer and at the same time invites her to go beyond the level of a simple motherly love. He trains his mother's faith in order that she may one day be qualified for her maternal role in the Church.

2. The Marriage Feast of Cana (John ii, 1–12)

We are told nothing of the parting between Jesus and Mary when Jesus left Nazareth to start preaching the Kingdom. Did this parting come about all at once, on a predetermined day, as happens when a son leaves his mother to begin a new life in another region? Or did it come about progressively, by short absences becoming more frequent and longer, until the thread of the joint life had become so tenuous that it only required a slight effort to break it? We do not know, but it seems that this second conjecture is more probable and that Jesus left his mother by degrees.

At the time of the marriage feast of Cana, Jesus had already met John the Baptist, had been baptized by him, and had chosen some disciples. The very simple words: '*The mother of Jesus was there*' recall and prepare the way for a similar sentence: 'But standing by the cross of Jesus was his mother' (John xix, 25). In fact, the episodes of the marriage at Cana and of Mary at the foot of the cross correspond one with the other. It is evident that the evangelist, in relating them, wishes to emphasize the link between them. Moreover, they are the only two passages in which the

1. Guardini.

evangelist speaks of the Virgin Mary—only two passages, but particularly meaningful if we remember the principles that guided St John in composing his Gospel. Writing a long time after the others, he carefully avoids treading the paths already trodden and relating the episodes already told. He is deliberately selective, as he himself admits (John xx, 30).

Let us note the restraint of the expression: 'the mother of Jesus'. The evangelist speaks of her with the same discretion as when speaking of himself. Their names are never mentioned.

'Jesus also was invited to the marriage.' In order to understand this episode we must bear the Passion of Jesus in mind. It is equally necessary to note that this is the first time that John meets Mary. Obviously, this meeting impresses itself on John's memory, since he gives it such prominent place in his Gospel.

'They have no wine', Mary says to Jesus. She has a woman's intuitive eye which takes in every detail of the arrangement of a meal. Her perception, refined by the purity of unselfish love and rendered still more penetrating by her own poverty, senses the possible humiliation of the hosts. The remark that Mary makes aside to Jesus, and that John is probably the only one to overhear, is not a request for a miracle. Mary has been living thirty years with Jesus without ever having seen a single miracle, so her mind is not conditioned to expect such a thing. She simply lets Jesus know of a situation she has just grasped and which arouses her sympathy. Her action is merely in the spirit of the life she has long been leading with her son.

'O woman, what have you to do with me? My hour has not yet come.' Jesus calls Mary 'woman' and not mother as he has been in the habit of doing. It is the term he uses when speaking to strange women (the Samaritan woman, the Canaanite woman, etc.). Indeed, the word 'woman' evokes in the Evangelist's mind the 'woman' of Gen. iii, 15. But one can guess the pain that Mary must have felt. No doubt she kept this word in her memory to reflect on until the day when she was to hear it again at the foot

of the cross, where she was probably to begin to understand its range.

'*What have you to do with me?*' It is very difficult to translate this Semitic expression, but it always signifies a refusal, a dismissal of something. His attendance at the marriage feast of Cana is at once the last joint action of a long family life and the first act of a new life in which Jesus is to act alone, engaged only in the work which the Heavenly Father has entrusted to him, in which he no longer has a family or an earthly mother. In any case, if we go by the exact meaning of the expression and judge it by the meaning it has in the Old Testament, Jesus definitely wishes to say to Mary that for the moment she has nothing in common with him. She is not on the same plane with him; she is thinking of the wine for the wedding feast while he wishes to give the true wine that is to be shed on Calvary, when his hour comes.

'*My hour has not yet come.*' Here it is a question, not of the hour to work a miracle but of the hour of the glorification of Jesus, that is to say, of his death and resurrection. This is always the meaning of the word 'hour' as spoken by Jesus (John vii, 30; viii, 20; xii, 23-27). The setting aside of Mary would be only temporary. She would find her place beside her son again when his hour came. In his reply Jesus made an appointment with his mother on Calvary. And this is why St John, who is the only evangelist to report the miracle of Cana, is also the only one who tells us of the presence of Mary at the foot of the cross. And he mentions her only in these two passages.

Mary's faith was put to the test. She had to renounce the rights which her position as his mother had given her till then. She had to accept the suffering of a bereaved heart. She had to prepare herself for that dread hour already foretold by Simeon. She did not understand the full meaning of Jesus' words, but she took them seriously since the words she addresses to the servants: 'Do whatever he tells you', the last words of Mary mentioned in the Gospel, show the faith she had in her son.

3. 'Here are my mother and my brothers!'

An *intrusion on the part of the family of Jesus* leads Jesus to reply to those who tell him of it: 'Here are my mother and my brothers! Whoever does the will of God is my brother, and sister and mother.'

This reply of Jesus presents two meanings:

(a) First, and more obviously, it means that Jesus in his messianic message does not recognize any right created by blood relationship to himself, in particular that of his mother. He only recognizes the ties of the spiritual relationship created by a common submission to the will of God. This first meaning of his words is clearly in the same spirit as the preceding replies made by Jesus to his mother. Jesus invites her to keep to the plane of faith. But if her consent was without hesitation, it was not without suffering.

(b) A second spiritual meaning arises from the first. If Mary was only his mother according to the flesh, she would not have any right to Jesus, any bond with him, any place in the kingdom. But we know full well that this faithful servant of the Lord is eminently of the spiritual family of Jesus because she has always done the will of God. We do not know if Mary perceived that this spiritual meaning was applicable to her life and to her soul; but it was above all the words of Jesus which left her in solitude. Thus her heart continued to widen and deepen through suffering.

4. The praise of the unknown woman (Luke xi, 27-28)

Jesus replies to the praise of this woman: 'Blessed rather are those who hear the word of God and keep it!'

This reply of Jesus to the words of the woman also has a two-fold meaning:

(a) A primary and obvious meaning is that in the messianic kingdom founded by Jesus no advantage on account of blood relationship is recognized, no glory is ever given to it. The only thing that counts is regard for the word of God and faithfulness in keeping it. Jesus remains faithful to the line of conduct which he began to lay down in his reply to his mother in the Temple at Jerusalem. He holds his mother firmly on the level of faith.

(b) A second, spiritual meaning arises from the first. Jesus does not say: 'You have no reason to praise my mother.' On the contrary, his words imply: If she merits this praise, it is not because she is my mother according to the flesh ('Blessed is the womb . . .') but because she has lived by the word of God which she has heard. It is the evangelist St Luke himself who related this little episode and who twice tells us that Mary kept in her heart the words of Jesus (according to which she lived). Hence we see that Jesus always affirms the superiority of the spiritual bonds formed by an obedient faith to God's word over the most sacred family bonds. Mary has become more of a mother to her son by obeying, believing and keeping the word of God than in giving him physical life.

If Mary heard this reply of Jesus, it must have impressed on her once more the high standard she was to maintain and the sentiments of faith she was to hold. Each word of Jesus went straight to the mark and found a profound echo in Mary's heart. Its effect completed the effect of the other words already heard, so through her suffering and deprivation of all human maternal joy, Mary became each day more fitted for her universal mission.

Each time Jesus encountered his mother during his public ministry, he demanded of her a greater spiritual response, the sacrificing of her rights as a mother. Mary had to be prepared to give up the normal reactions of a mother and to accept loneliness and further separation, for this was to be her part in the Redeemer's work.

V. THE TRIAL OF BLOOD

1. *The Prophecy of Simeon*

The prophecy of Simeon confronted Mary early on with the

mystery of the cross. After the old man had addressed words so full of hope to Joseph and Mary that they were taken aback, he turned abruptly to Mary alone and all at once said: 'Behold, this child is set for the fall and rising of many in Israel, and for a sign that is spoken against, and a sword will pierce your own soul also' (Luke ii, 35).

Simeon's prophecy shows Mary the meaning of her whole life. Jesus has been born of her in order to die on the cross and be a sign that will be spoken against. And her destiny is modelled on that of her son.

The prophecy remains engraved on Mary's heart and grows in strength with each new trial she undergoes. When a future suffering is inevitable, it casts its shadow over all the joys of life, and sullies them. The sword is to become a daily reality, piercing her soul more and more. On this day Mary discovered the vital meaning of her vocation, and the fact that she remembered this incident so vividly shows the impression it made on her.

2. *The Meeting on Calvary*

'When Jesus saw his mother and the beloved disciple standing near, he said to his mother, "Woman, behold your son!" Then he said to his disciple, "Behold, your mother!" And from that hour the disciple took her to his own home' (John xix, 25-27).

These words of Jesus have often been interpreted as the normal reaction of a dying son who foresees the loneliness which his mother will have to face in the future. But this explanation is unacceptable for many reasons.

Was it really necessary to make special arrangements to help a mother who had been left alone for the past three years, and who has numerous relatives to help her in her loneliness? And Jesus, after reaching the climax of his redemptive mission, the 'day' for which he came, the 'hour' for which his Father sent him, surely would not choose this solemn moment to settle a purely family question which could have been settled long before if necessary.

Moreover, St John is anxious in this chapter to show that the prophecies have been fulfilled, and after this episode he adds: 'After that, Jesus, knowing that all was now finished . . .' Thus, to his mind and to the mind of Jesus, the declaration made to Mary and the disciple is the final conclusion of the mission entrusted to him by the Eternal Father.

The word 'woman'—a word Christ did not normally use when speaking of his mother—shows that he was going beyond the level of mere human family relations.

Moreover, if we read the text carefully we can see that it is not primarily Mary who is entrusted to John, but rather John to Mary. Jesus is thereby assigning a real mission to Mary. He entrusts 'the disciple' to her in the same hour in which he redeems mankind. What is more, he does not ask her to act as a mother, he makes her a mother. He does not say: 'Woman, look on him in future as your son', but: 'Woman, behold, your son.' He does not say to John: 'Regard her as your mother', but: 'Behold, your mother!' These words of Jesus have creative power and they effect what they mean. They make the disciple the true son of Mary, and Mary the true mother of John.[1]

But at the same time these words ask Mary to consummate the sacrifice of her earthly nature.

The words of Jesus to Mary and John assume their full meaning only when related to all the other words heard by Mary during the course of her life. When she consented to become the mother of Jesus on the day of the annunciation, she could not guess the full extent of this motherhood: that in becoming the mother of one person she was to become the mother of all. But she could only become the mother of all at the price of an exceptional growth in her power to love, and consequently of a ruthless stripping of everything purely human in her love as a mother. That was why the Holy Spirit espoused her in faith, and why the motherhood of Mary was sorrowful from the very beginning.

1. This already began to be so from the time of the annunciation.

She learned from Simeon that a sword of sorrow would pierce her soul. She also learned from the child Jesus himself that his heart belonged only to his heavenly Father. At Cana, Jesus urged her to put herself on the right level for sharing in his work. She understood too that the only relationship he recognized was a spiritual one. By this deprivation Mary was prepared to understand that her motherhood was above all a spiritual one.

On Calvary Mary realizes the greatness of her task. Instead of being tempted to concentrate on herself and her own immense sorrow as a mother, she must detach herself from her sorrow in order to take over and adopt the whole human race as her children in the person of John. She is at the foot of the cross as the mother of all mankind, offering her only son for the redemption of her sons by adoption. She is the descendant of Eve, the 'woman' who is to restore in her own person God's original plan.

Conclusion

WE can certainly say that Mary was called to be the mother of all, and she was formed in faithfulness by the Holy Spirit to become 'mother' in an ever deeper and wider sense.

On this road of motherhood, we can distinguish three stages, three panels of a triptych.

1. *The first stage* extends from the immaculate conception to the annunciation. We have no historical data about this whole period. We do not know Mary's parents. We can be sure that they were saints if they received such a privileged child from God. The Church has rightly canonized them and given them names by which to be honoured. We know nothing about the childhood of Mary except that she definitely was not presented at the age of three, for the service of the Temple was neither a kindergarten nor a boarding-school for girls. But the liturgical feast of the Presentation of Mary in the Temple has a much more profound meaning than the mere commemoration of an historical fact. It expresses all that careful preparation of Mary's soul which inclined her to make her life a spontaneous and continual 'presentation' of her whole being to God.

But we do know the essentials of that first period of Mary's life because the angel Gabriel, Elizabeth, and Mary herself tell us the results. Mary is full of grace; the Lord is with her; she is blessed among women. The Almighty has done great things in her. Being thus prepared, she is able to receive the angel and understand his message. In short, during those years Mary was being formed by the Holy Spirit to become the mother of Jesus. She receives the gift of the divine motherhood as a seed. But she does not and cannot know that as mother of Jesus she is also the mother of a multitude of souls, and that from the time of his conception Jesus is inseparable from his brothers.

2. This is what she is to learn in *the second stage* of her life, the period between the two annunciations—the visit of the angel Gabriel and the words of Jesus on the cross. This heart, this mother's heart entirely filled with love for her son, must be worked upon by God with the means by which he tests and strengthens faithfulness. Of course, there is no self-love in Mary's love for Jesus and her love as a mother does not need to be purified, but like every human love it needs to grow. This heart must expand little by little to become capable of embracing so many other children. And it is the Holy Spirit that is to instruct it in the spiritual detachment and sacrifice which such mother-hood demands. Here we can see the sufferings Mary encountered during her life. They are there at the very beginning, from the time Simeon's prophecy introduces the sword of sorrow into Mary's life. Jesus himself continues this work of harrowing her soul by the disconcerting words that mark each of his public encounters with her. All these words invite her to leave the level of a simple human mother's love, in itself limited, to pass to the level of a universal, supernatural love. And each stage of progress on this road is made at the cost of a progressive detachment from self.

Having faithfully accepted this long and painful process to form her Mary arrives at the foot of the cross to hear the second annunciation. She is to discover what being the mother of Jesus means. To be the mother of Jesus is to have a heart large enough to receive the whole world, all the brothers of her first-born son.

3. Here *the third stage* begins. Living in the Church that is being founded and peopled. Mary is to discover in herself great reserves of a mother's love. She is the mother of a Mystical Body that is continually growing, the mother of children born cease-lessly to grace; the mother who has never ceased bringing children into the world and bringing them up at the cost of her very life-blood. Is not this the reason why she weeps and asks people to do penance whenever she appears on earth? Mary is in

fact still carrying on the mission that was hers during the earthly life of Jesus. She was associated in the mission of her son then, and it was a sorrowful mission. The cross was always in view for Jesus and the sword of sorrow was always before Mary. She is still the mother of sinners, that is why she is sorrowful. But at the same time the Church is becoming increasingly aware of Mary's place in her growth. In other words, Mary's vocation is still developing as the Church develops. And in fact a vocation never ceases, because one who hears the call of God is to discover that death is only a stage.

When St Thérèse of the Child Jesus said that she wished to spend her heaven doing good on earth, she realized that her vocation would continue to grow unceasingly after her death. Mary had already seen this, and the Church continually discovers it anew in contemplating her mystery.

For each person God has a plan which becomes ever clearer in its scope and ambition. But when he comes before God this person is made to realize that his task is still not finished and that God expects a generosity of heart after the pattern of his own.

IV
Jesus Trains the Apostles in Faith

Introduction

JESUS took his apostles from the ordinary run of Jewish people. They were 'good Israelites' who knew their Bible, and above all knew the Lord. But they were not at all interested in academic arguments or quibbles of the Pharisees. They were neither scholars nor intellectuals. In fact, they could neither read nor write. Whatever they knew, they had learnt by hearing.

Most of them were manual workers—fishermen from Lake Tiberias like Peter, Andrew, James and John—and they were of the same social class as Jesus himself, from the country round Nazareth. Some of them were even relatives of his.

Jesus chose them deliberately from this social layer: 'I chose you' (John xv, 16). One day he was to explain the deep motive of this choice. 'I thank thee, Father, Lord of heaven and earth, that thou hast hidden these things from the wise and understanding and revealed them to babes' (Matt. xi, 25). It was not necessary for the disciples to be rich in superficial knowledge but it was necessary that they should be open to the influence of their master.

St Paul discerns a similar predilection on God's part. 'But God chose what is foolish in the world to shame the wise, God chose what is weak in the world to shame the strong, God chose what is low and despised in the world, even things that are not, to bring to nothing things that are, so that no human being might boast in the presence of God' (1 Cor. i, 27-29).

The whole life of Jesus with his apostles can be regarded as a continual education on his part. They had no books to read or documents to write. During a life together which Jesus knew would be very brief, it was necessary for him to give the apostles the essentials they needed in order to found the Church, and the essentials the Church would need until the end of time. Of course, there was doctrine, but more important was the spirit, and above all, faith.

Jesus formed the faith of his disciples, not by enriching their memory with a coherent body of ideas, but by starting out from what the Twelve already were, with their knowledge and their Jewish faith, and by subjecting them to an active teaching.

Their practical spirit was ready to accept such a teaching in which parables provided food for the mind and actions or miracles the practical application.

But if the apostles were to be capable of establishing the Church, they needed above all to have faith, and this is why Jesus was to set about educating them patiently in this faith.

12.

Jesus Initiates His Apostles into Knowledge of the Holy Trinity

I. THE REVELATION OF THE FATHER

THE apostles knew the Lord, the God of Abraham, of Isaac and of Jacob. It is of him that Jesus speaks to the Twelve. Or rather, he himself speaks to this God, but in doing so calls him by a new name, that of Father. And it is here that Jesus employs an active pedagogic method. He makes his apostles witnesses of his filial life prayer. To this name of Father he joins a possessive pronoun: he says '*my* Father', and this gives the appellation a particularly personal meaning and emphasis. What is more, he teaches his apostles that his Father is also their Father. He teaches them to live as children of the Father.

1. If we read the Gospels with an open mind, the first thing that impresses us is *the frequent or rather constant, use of the name of Father*. There is nothing systematic in the message of Jesus. It is by his own spontaneous attitude that he reveals the Father. He lives in such intimacy with him that when he opens his mouth he speaks of him spontaneously. He always has his name on the tip of his tongue because his heart is so full of love for him. 'But I do as the Father has commanded me, so that the world may know that I love the Father' (John xiv, 31; cf. viii, 29).

How many texts of this kind we find in the Gospels, spontaneous, incisive words, expressing a constant love, like a subterranean river that comes to the surface again and again! Jesus prays to his Father at his baptism (Luke iii, 21), and when choosing his apostles (Luke vi, 12). When the disciples return from their

first apostolic journey, Jesus rejoices and cries: 'I thank thee,
Father . . .' (Matt. xi, 25).

The will of his Father is the ultimate explanation that Jesus
gives to those who show astonishment at his behaviour. Why, for
instance, does he limit his activities to the narrow confines of
Palestine? 'I was sent only to the lost sheep of the house of Israel'
(Matt. xv, 24), he replies. Why does he consort with sinners, tax
collectors and people who have somehow gone wrong? No
doubt because they are stray sheep, but also because: 'All that the
Father gives me will come to me; and him who comes to me I
will not cast out. For I have come down from heaven, not to do
my own will, but the will of him who sent me' (John vi, 37).

Why does he, contrary to good sense and the warnings of his
best friends, make that last journey to Jerusalem and the death
which awaits him there? 'Shall I not drink the cup which the
Father has given me?' (John xviii, 11).

For his disciples all this is a permanent object-lesson, a continual education.

2. *The tone of Jesus when he speaks to his Father is that of an
eye-witness who recalls him.* Jesus in fact says: 'I came from the
Father and have come into the world' (John xvi, 28). More than
once he makes an explicit allusion to his eternal existence:
'Before Abraham was, I am' (John viii, 58); 'But you have not
known him; I know him' (John viii, 55).

How many of the sayings of Jesus stand out in a new and
moving relief if we understand them as the echo of an eternal life
of contemplation! All things—the flowers of the fields, the birds of
the air—speak to Jesus of the greatness, the incessant action of the
Father. A meeting with a child evokes for him a vision of the
angels in heaven contemplating the face of the Father which Jesus
seems to see reflected in the face of the child.

He sees the action of the Father in a disciple's faith: 'No one
can come to me unless the Father who sent me draws him' (John
vi, 44); and when Peter proclaims him to be the Christ, the son

of the living God, Jesus replies: 'Blessed are you, Simon Bar-Jona! For flesh and blood has not revealed this to you, but my Father who is in heaven' (Matt. xvi, 17). Indeed, the prayer that Jesus addresses aloud to his Father sometimes seems to be the last sentence of an interior dialogue: 'Father, I thank thee that thou hast heard me. I know that thou hearest me always' (John xi, 41–42).

3. *The bond that unites Christ to his Father constitutes the unity of his being*. When Jesus says: 'I live because of the Father' (John vi, 57), he thereby reveals to his disciples the secret of himself. He lives only by virtue of the life received from the Father; he lives only for the Father. This explains how Jesus can be at once completely humble and completely self-assured. His humility does not restrict his personality, but stretches it to its full extent, because it is inspired by love.

Jesus often emphasizes to his apostles the unity that exists between his Father and himself: 'Yet I am not alone, for the Father is with me' (John xvi, 32; cf. viii, 16); 'If you knew me, you would know my Father also' (John viii, 19); 'I and the Father are one' (John x, 30); 'The Father is in me and I am in the Father' (John x, 38).

4. *His bond with the Father also unifies the life and action of Jesus*. All this action is contemplative. Love of the Father inspires the whole ministry of Jesus: his preaching is not an exposition of dry morality, but preaching of the Father, and the precepts of the Sermon on the Mount are all centred on the Father. It is because of this love that he consents to confine his public ministry within the narrow boundaries of Palestine. It is for this love too, that he consents to face the failure and shame of Calvary—a consent which costs him overwhelming agony.

We have only to read John xii, 23–28, or the story of the agony in Gethsemane in order to see what very severe demands his love of the Father can make on him.

5. But while showing his apostles the personal bonds which

bind him to the Father and thus making them want to know the Father ('Lord, show us the Father, and we shall be satisfied', says Philip in John xiv, 8), *Jesus teaches his apostles that God is their Father.* He teaches them to pray to the Father (Luke xi, 1-13) by giving them in the Lord's Prayer, that epitome of all prayers, a magnificent lesson on balanced prayer, entirely directed towards God yet not forgetful of the humble needs of the physical and spiritual life. How can we ever again think of God otherwise than as a good Father, mindful of the cries of his children? 'Or what man of you, if his son asks him for bread, will give him a stone? ... If you then, who are evil, know how to give good gifts to your children, how much more will your Father who is in heaven give good things to those who ask him!' (Matt. vii, 9, 11).

He teaches them to trust in the loving providence of the Father (Matt. vi, 25-34), and more especially to abandon themselves to his mercy. The parable of the prodigal son, which we read in the fifteenth chapter of St Luke, draws a particularly moving picture of the Father. In it Jesus shows the father's respect for the liberty of the son, and his faithful affection in spite of the son's failures ('But while he was yet at a distance, his father saw him and had compassion, and ran and embraced him and kissed him'). And the father is so merciful that he reinstates his erring son completely.

6. *This education bears fruit with the apostles.* They speak with immense respect of the heavenly Father. St James tells us: 'Every good endowment and every perfect gift is from above, coming down from the Father of lights with whom there is no variation or shadow due to change' (James i, 17). St Peter says: 'And if you invoke as Father him who judges each one impartially according to his deeds, conduct yourselves with fear throughout the time of your exile' (1 Peter i, 17).

They rival each other in emphasizing the reality of our sonship. God has not only called himself Father that we may call him by that name but he has made us his real children: 'To all who receive him, who believed in his name, he gave power to become children of God' (John i, 12); 'See what love the Father has given us, that we should be called children of God; and so we are' (1 John iii, 1); 'For this reason I bow my knees before the Father, from whom every family in heaven and on earth is named' (Eph. iii, 14-15).

This is the vital discovery that the apostles made in their common life with Jesus and under his patient guidance. The omnipotent God whom they worshipped under the name of Yahweh or the Lord is really the Father of their master, Jesus Christ, and their Father, and the grace of redemption which Jesus has brought them consists above all in this revelation that they are truly children of the heavenly Father.

II. THE REVELATION OF JESUS, THEIR SAVIOUR

How did Jesus reveal himself to his apostles? He did not give them a conceptual teaching *ex cathedra*. Instead, he made himself known to them progressively by acting before them (*'coepit facere'*) with the very dynamism of his being, adapting this revelation to their ability to receive it at the time.

1. *Jesus begins by curing and saving the body.* The Gospels are full of stories of miracles, and we feel that the apostles had their fill of them. Why did Jesus work these miracles? No doubt it was out of kindness towards the sick and suffering, but it was more especially for the training of his apostles. Each miracle that Jesus works is a lesson for his apostles. This pedagogic intention is often emphasized—at Cana, for instance: 'This, the first of his signs, Jesus did at Cana in Galilee, and manifested his glory; and his disciples believed in him' (John ii, 11).

When Jesus cures the man born blind, the apostles ask him: 'Rabbi, who sinned, this man or his parents, that he was born blind?' Jesus answers: 'It was not that this man sinned, or his parents, but that the works of God might be made manifest in him' (John ix, 2-3).

When Jesus is told that Lazarus is ill, he declares: 'This illness is not unto death; it is for the glory of God, so that the Son of God may be glorified by means of it' (John xi, 4). And he deliberately delays: 'So when he heard that he was ill, he stayed two days longer in the place where he was' (John xi, 6). And after Lazarus has died, Jesus announces his death to his disciples, but adds: 'And for your sake I am glad that I was not there, so that you may believe' (John xi, 14-15).

This is a clue which enables us to understand the actions of Jesus. In curing people, our Lord has his apostles and the training of their faith in mind. Hence, he cures the sick of mind and body, the lepers (Luke xvii, 11-19), the blind (Matt. xx, 34), and so on. But he takes care that they profit spiritually from this cure, for he asks them to believe in him. And so in this it is not only the sick people but also the apostles whom Jesus has in mind.

2. In the eyes of Jesus, the body is not of great importance in itself. *The entire human being, body and soul, is the object of his compassion.* One day, a paralytic is brought to him, let down through a roof, and Jesus cures him in body and soul, at the same time pointing out that the healing of the body signifies the healing of the soul.

How often we find Jesus curing someone of his grave sin, but making the gift of his love and salvation to the whole person, body and soul. He can only make this gift, however, to someone who feels the need of being saved and knows himself to be poor, sick and wretched. Many of the sayings of Jesus can only be understood if interpreted as a permanent teaching where repetition plays an important role. 'For God sent the Son into the world, not to condemn the world, but that the world might be saved through him' (John iii, 17); 'For I came not to call the righteous, but sinners' (Matt. ix, 13); 'There will be more joy in heaven over one sinner who repents than over ninety-nine righteous persons who need no repentance' (Luke xv, 7); 'There is joy before the angels of God over one sinner who repents' (Luke xv, 10). And referring to Zacchaeus: 'The Son of man came to seek and to save the lost' (Luke xix, 10).

Similarly, in the parable of the Pharisee and the tax-collector he tells of 'some who trusted in themselves that they were righteous and despised others' (Luke xviii, 9).

The mercy that Jesus shows publicly to the 'woman of the city': 'Your sins are forgiven' (Luke vii, 48); and the woman taken in adultery: 'Neither do I condemn you; go, and do not sin again' (John viii, 11), are to be understood in the same light.

During all the years spent with his apostles, Jesus kept telling them that he had come to save those who felt the need of being saved, and he very often bestowed the gift of salvation on such persons before his apostles' eyes.

3. At the time of the passion and resurrection the apostles experienced *the mercy of their Lord* still more directly. He is about to leave them to their resources in order that they may experience their own utter inadequacy, but he does so with immense kindness. Even with Judas he shows no harshness. He pleads with his heavenly Father for his persecutors: 'Father, forgive them, for they know not what they do.' He overcomes his own agony to promise heaven to the good thief, his companion in torture who is full of misery because of his misused life that it is too late to amend. Now the thief can only utter a supplication. And he is, in a sense, the most completely saved of beings, for he is the only person to whom heaven was promised at the very moment of death, *and heaven with Jesus.*

After the resurrection, Jesus chooses to appear first to Mary Magdalen and to Peter. When he seeks out the apostles who have fled, he does not make them the slightest reproach, and twice he says to them 'Peace be with you'.

Jesus complies with the demand of Thomas, who has obstinately disbelieved the witnesses of the resurrection. He takes Thomas's hand in his and makes him touch his wounds. To Peter, who denied him thrice, Jesus restores his dignity and prerogatives.

Having thrice asked for and received the assurance of his love, he confides his Church to him.

4. In short, as the years of common life with Jesus passed, it became ever more clear to the apostles that the essential definition of their Lord was: *He who has come to save.*

After the ascension of the Lord and the descent of the Holy Spirit, they were more capable of understanding in this same light certain facts concerning the childhood of Jesus; more capable of grasping his mission of salvation as a whole. Thus they learned that the name of Jesus had been given to him intentionally because, as the angel had said to Joseph: 'He will save his people from their sins' (Matt. i, 21). They also understand why Jesus had known poor and precarious conditions in his life ever since birth. It was so that no individual could ever doubt that Jesus had come for him personally. The poorest person in the world, one most accustomed to lacking everything, upon seeing such destitution would easily understand that this little child had come into the world for him, too. And this is what the shepherds, the only invited guests on the night of the nativity, were meant to grasp. All people who work with their hands, all people dedicated to monotonous and lowly work, were represented there by them. The poverty and privation of Jesus were the sign of their salvation, the sign by which to recognize their saviour: 'For to you is born this day in the city of David a *saviour*, who is Christ the Lord. And this will be a sign for you: you will find a babe wrapped in swaddling cloths and lying in a manger' (Luke ii, 11-12). Some time later it was the turn of the wise men, the first representatives of the pagan peoples who were to be saved by Jesus. They represented all those who look for a divine light down the ages; all those who thirst for a God whom they do not know; all those who wander long in a spiritual desert.

Certainly, after our Lord's departure, his mission seemed to the apostles more and more a mission of salvation. This mission was admirably summed up for them in the name that had been given to Jesus: 'For he will save his people from their sins'. This is why the mission of the apostles consisted essentially in preaching this very name of Jesus.

When Peter and John cure the lame man at the Temple gate called 'Beautiful', they do so 'in the name of Jesus Christ of Nazareth' (Acts iii, 6). Then they explain the meaning of their words and actions to the crowd that has gathered: 'And his name, by faith in his name, has made this man strong whom you see and know' (Acts iii, 16).

This is also a dominant note in the teaching of St Paul: 'For the grace of God has appeared for the salvation of all men . . . awaiting our blessed hope, the appearing of the glory of our great God and *saviour* Jesus Christ' (Titus ii, 11, 13); 'But when the goodness and loving kindness of God *our saviour* appeared, he saved us . . . in virtue of his own mercy' (Titus iii, 4-5; cf. Eph. ii, 4-5; Gal. ii, 20).

This is the dominant idea that sums up the mission of Christ in the minds of the apostles. Or rather, this is the most essential feature of his being as outlined by our Lord himself to his apostles, in order that they, in their turn, might describe to their successors the Lord whom they have known.

III. THE REVELATION OF THE HOLY SPIRIT

1. *The Old Testament had certainly prepared the mentality of the apostles for the coming of the Holy Spirit.* The words of the prophet Isaiah will have dwelt in their memories: 'There shall come forth a shoot from the stump of Jesse . . . And the spirit of the Lord shall rest upon him' (Is. xi, 1-2); 'Behold my servant . . . my chosen, in whom my soul delights; I have put my spirit upon him' (Is. xlii, 1): 'The spirit of the Lord is upon me; he has sent me to bind up the broken-hearted, to proclaim liberty to the captives' (Is. lxi, 1).

Similarly, the apostles present at the baptism of Jesus by John the Baptist hear the voice of the heavenly Father recalling the prophecy of Isaiah xlii, 1 (Matt. xii, 18). In the same way, they hear Jesus, in the synagogue at Nazareth, expounding the prophecy of Isaiah lxi, 1 (Luke iv, 17-21). They often likewise hear him speaking of the Holy Spirit (Matt. xii, 28-32; John iii, 5-8).

But all this was very confused at first in the apostles' minds. Jesus did not really and truly reveal the Holy Spirit to them. He revealed himself to them, and he revealed his Father. But he promised the Holy Spirit, and finally he sent him. The Holy Spirit then revealed himself by throwing a new light on the Father and the Son.

2. Certain mysterious words of Jesus are the key to *the promise of the Holy Spirit made by Jesus* and *the revelation of himself which the Holy Spirit is to make*. Actually, Jesus says to his apostles: 'Nevertheless I tell you the truth: it is good for you that I go away, for if I do not go away, the Counsellor will not come to you; but if I go, I will send him to you . . . When the Spirit of truth comes, he will guide you into all the truth' (John xvi, 7, 13). 'And I will pray the Father, and he will give you another Counsellor, to be with you for ever . . . But, the Counsellor, the Holy Spirit, whom the Father will send in my name, he will teach you all things, and bring to your remembrance all that I have said to you' (John xiv, 16, 26).

Why and how could it be good for them that the Lord should go away? Might it not have been better if he had remained with his young Church, giving it the benefit of his infallible and appropriate teaching, the magnetism of his physical presence, the might of his miraculous powers?

Let us reflect and ask ourselves what fate we would have meted out to Christ if we had known him as they did. Because we are carnal and our life of faith difficult, we would inevitably have regarded him as a wonder-worker from whom to expect material food, material graces, cures, the raising from the dead of someone dear to us, the solution of problems, or the arbitration of disputes. We would spontaneously have seen the man in Jesus, and not the risen God made man.

Let us recall the difficulty Jesus experienced in making the invisible mysteries meaningful to Nicodemus (John iii), the Samaritan woman (John iv), and those for whom he had multiplied the loaves (Mark viii, 1-21). Let us recall the effort of Jesus to make the paralytic, who only expected a physical cure, understand that the essential thing was to be cured in both body and soul; or again, to make Martha, who expected the physical resurrection of Lazarus, understand the essential fact that Jesus himself was the resurrection and the life. At each miracle of healing Jesus required the person healed to make an act of faith, because it is by faith that we pass from the carnal to the spiritual plane. And the apostles were always tacitly invited, together with those to whom Jesus was speaking, to follow this way of faith. To be sure, Jesus willingly consented to heal the sick or raise the dead body, but more often than not it was in order that the physical miracle should be a sign of the spiritual miracle. And he asked the person he was about to heal—and with him the apostles—'Do you believe?', so that an act of faith should accompany or follow the miracle.

But in spite of three years of such lessons, and in spite even of the passion and resurrection, the apostles still did not understand, and we recall how they asked Jesus almost piteously on the very morning of the ascension: 'Lord, will you at this time restore the kingdom to Israel?' (Acts i, 6).

This is why Jesus, in order to force them to live by faith, did his work at this stage in two phases, each obviously closely linked with the other:

(a) He began by depriving them of his presence, and gave them the lesson of the ascension: 'It is good for you that I go away.'

(b) Then he sent them the Holy Spirit to help them to live in faith, teach them all things, and recall and clarify for them all the things Jesus had said.

Certainly Jesus had said all that was necessary, but it was essential that he should go away in order that his apostles might be confirmed in their faith, and it was the Holy Spirit who was to help them on this last stage. He was to make them look into their own hearts and discover Christ permanently present in them. The Holy Spirit came, not to replace the personal presence of Jesus but to realize it in a new, spiritual and final way. The presence of the Holy Spirit is inseparable from that of Jesus. As St Paul says, the Holy Spirit is the spirit of Jesus. This was the meaning of Jesus' promise: 'And I will pray the Father, and he will give you another Counsellor, to be with you for ever, *even the Spirit of truth . . . you know him, for he dwells with you, and will be in you.* I will not leave you desolate. I will come to you . . . you will see me' (John xii, 16-19).

Pentecost truly marks an epoch-making date in the spiritual growth of the apostles. The effect of this transformation is especially visible in Peter. Before pentecost Christ is beside him and very near to him. After pentecost Christ is in him and works upon him from within. Before pentecost he loved Christ with the passion (and instability) of a human love, but this love was not to save him from the fear of persecution and from denying his Lord. After pentecost, Christ is in Peter, and the latter can no longer remain silent and keep the Gospel to himself ('*non possumus non loqui*'). And he is to write later from personal experience: 'If you are reproached for the name of Christ, you are blessed, because the spirit of glory and of God rests upon you' (1 Peter iv, 14).

The book of Acts, which can be called the Gospel of the Holy Spirit, shows this continual action of the Holy Spirit in the disciples of Jesus. The deacon Stephen repeats in the course of his martyrdom the very words Jesus had spoken in his passion: 'Behold, I see the heavens opened, and the Son of man standing at the right hand of God . . . Lord, do not hold this sin against them' (Acts vii, 56, 60). It costs Stephen no effort to say this: he is 'filled with the Holy Spirit'. This illustrates the promise of Jesus: 'When they deliver you up, do not be anxious how you are to speak or what you are to say; for what you are to say will be given to you in that hour; for it is not you who speak, but the Spirit of your Father speaking through you' (Matt. x, 19-20).

Christ *has revealed himself* as the Word Incarnate, the Son of God made man. He is 'the door' by which we enter into the Trinity. *He reveals the Father:* 'The only Son, who is in the bosom of the Father, he has made him known' (John i, 18). *He sends his Holy Spirit.*

The Holy Spirit *reveals himself* and at the same time *brings a new revelation of the Father* ('the Spirit of God') *and of Christ* ('the Spirit of Christ') (Rom. viii, 9).

The apostles are to have the experience which Mary had had before them—that of the indwelling of the Holy Spirit—but had been unable to put in writing. They are to discover and explain that the Holy Spirit is the author of the growth of their faith. St Paul is to write, for example, that no one can say 'Jesus is Lord', that is, make the elementary act of faith required of catechumens in the early Church, 'except by the Holy Spirit' (1 Cor. vii, 3). He will say repeatedly that the Holy Spirit dwells in the soul of the Christian (1 Cor. iii, 16-17, vi, 9-11, 19-20; 2 Cor. vi, 5-11; Tim. i, 14); that he gives peace and joy (Rom. xv, 13); sanctifies (2 Thess. ii, 13-14); is the source of spiritual liberty (Gal. iv, 3-7; Rom. viii, 12-17, 26-27); and is the source of love (Rom. v, 5). St Paul certainly makes it clear that his ministry as an apostle is constantly animated by the Holy Spirit (1 Thess. i, 2-7; 1 Cor. ii, 1-5, 12-13; Rom. xv, 15-19).

And in the Acts of the Apostles we see clearly that each impetus to the growth of the nascent Church stems from the Holy Spirit:

(a) Peter's first sermon after Pentecost (ii, 14);

(b) the preaching of Peter to the Samaritans (viii, 15-20);

(c) the decision to preach to the Gentiles (viii, 29-39);

(d) the decision to receive the centurion Cornelius into the Church (x, 19–38, 44–47; xi, 12–17);

(e) the choice of Paul and Barnabas to carry the Gospel message abroad (xiii, 2–4, 9, 52);

(f) and the increase in the number of the faithful is always indicated as the work of the Holy Spirit (ix, 31; xv, 8, 28).

On reading the Acts or the epistles, we understand by the hundreds of texts reporting the action of the Holy Spirit, that the apostles have discovered by daily experience that all spiritual growth is the work of the Spirit.

13

Jesus Teaches His Apostles to Grow in Hope

WE can follow Jesus' training of the apostles in the virtue of hope in two main directions: hope in Jesus himself, and hope in the kingdom of God.

Of course this distinction is clearly arbitrary, and the revelation that Jesus makes of himself is inseparable from his revelation of the kingdom, as we shall often have occasion to point out. But our sole aim in making this distinction here is to help us to go forward in our discovery of the truth.

I. HOPE IN THE PERSON OF JESUS

The apostles knew the history of Abraham. They also knew the history of the people of Israel, which is one long education in hope and fidelity.

But they had to be formed by Jesus:

(a) in order that they should understand in their hearts what they already knew only in their minds;

(b) and more especially in order that they should apply to Jesus himself the confidence which they placed in the omnipotence of God, and should discover little by little that with our Lord nothing is impossible.

This was the education instilled into the apostles by Jesus during their three years of life together. We cannot distinguish the stages of growth of the apostles' hope or even discern how far they had progressed in it by the end of the public life of Jesus, because the circumstances of the passion of Jesus seemed to sweep everything away. It is certain, however, that the Holy Spirit completed the assimilation by the apostles of all that Jesus had taught them about hope.

But what we can do is to discern the method of training used by Jesus. The evangelists' accounts of the miracles worked by Christ show us this vividly. They reveal that Jesus, when working a miracle, always thought of the apostles who were looking on and listening and had to be trained in hope. Moreover, in many of the stories two superimposed elements can be distinguished:

(a) the facts themselves and their sequence;

(b) a certain setting of the scene by Jesus, which accentuates the conditions in which the miracles are effected, with the result that these strike the minds of the apostles and educate them in hope.

1. *The raising of the daughter of Jairus* (Mark v, 22–43)

Jairus comes to Jesus. His daughter is at the point of death, and falling at the feet of Jesus he begs him come and cure her.

What is the value of the confidence that Jairus places in Jesus? Does he take him for an ordinary healer? Does he take him for a wonder-worker? Does he take him for the Messiah? Does he take him for the Son of God? We do not know. However great the confidence Jairus has in Jesus, the latter is going to try him in order to purify his confidence, to make it grow, and to teach Jairus the dimensions of supernatural hope. The lesson given to Jairus will benefit the apostles, for it is of them and their formation that Jesus is thinking.

Let us put ourselves in Jairus's place, and also in the place of the apostles who share the anxiety of the unhappy father. The matter is urgent; the child is at the point of death. At such moments, time is precious; seconds count. Now comes the first trial: the huge crowd presses round Jesus and impedes his progress. Four times (v, 21, 24, 27, 31) Mark stresses the density of the crowd.

Then comes the episode of the woman with the flow of blood to delay Jesus still more. Mark recounts this with humour: 'And there was a woman who had had a flow of blood for twelve years, and who had suffered much under many physicians, and had spent all that she had, and was no better but rather grew worse . . .' Luke the doctor, in his story of this miracle (viii, 40-56), is much more respectful towards the profession. But Mark, by his little rub at the doctors, emphasizes the gravity of the ailment from which the woman is suffering. She is cured by simply touching the garment of Jesus, who could now have passed on and so saved time out of consideration for the anxious Jairus and the impatient apostles, who were waiting for him. But no, he stops, turns round, looks about him attentively, and asks 'Who touched my garments?' What a question! In a crowd as dense as that anyone could touch the garments of Jesus. The disciples, exasperated by the loss of time and the futile question, say to Jesus impatiently: 'You see the crowd pressing around you, and yet you say, "Who touched me?" ' (Luke puts these words on the lips of Peter). But Jesus takes no notice of the disciples' impertinence and continues to look around him until the woman, feeling she has been discovered, comes forward frightened and trembling to tell him the whole truth.

Jairus and the apostles, devoured with impatience, hear the lesson that emerges from the episode when Jesus says to the woman: 'Daughter, your faith has made you well; go in peace, and be healed of your disease.'

All this talk has taken so much time that what everyone had feared from the beginning happens. Someone comes from the house of Jairus and says: 'Your daughter is dead. Why trouble the teacher any further?'

All human hope is dead. Now is the time for supernatural hope. Jesus says to Jairus: 'Do not fear, only believe.'

This whole story shows exactly how Jesus acted. The miracle is one thing, but the teaching is another thing, and much more important. All the words and actions of Jesus here have the purpose of forming the hope of his disciples. He waited until it was too late so that the supernatural hope, rising from the depths of radical human helplessness, should blossom in reliance on the power of God that shines forth in Christ and calls the child back from the gates of death.

2. *The faith of the Canaanite woman* (Matt. xv, 21–28)

This woman approaches Jesus and says to him: 'Have mercy on me, O Lord, Son of David; my daughter is serverely possessed by a demon.' What is this woman's degree of hope? For whom does she take Jesus? Certainly she calls him 'Son of David', but what does this title mean to a non-Israelite? Jesus will educate the hope of this woman by obliging her, by successive tests, to rise above herself. The apostles will become involved and subconsciously accept what Jesus says to the woman. And when they try to brush off this stranger they will learn to what heights of faith and humility she can rise.

The woman now appeals to Jesus, and in the eastern manner, repeats the same petition again and again with a great flow of words.

The first test: Jesus does not reply and continues on his way as if he had heard nothing.

The woman continues her entreaties. The apostles enter on the scene and, encouraged by the pretended indifference of Jesus, think to back it up by crushing the poor woman before him. 'Send her away', they say, 'for she is crying after us.' The woman refuses to be disconcerted by their hostility, clears the barrier of this test, and continues her entreaties.

Jesus himself imposes a third test, that of refusal: he cannot do anything for her, she is not of the chosen people. 'I was sent only to the lost sheep of the house of Israel.' The woman clears this third barrier, and prostrating herself before Jesus, says, 'Lord, help me!'

Jesus thereupon imposes his last test, going to the length of an insult by comparing the woman to a dog. (We know that in the

Bible, and everywhere in the East, the name 'dog' is the worst possible insult). 'It is not fair', says Jesus, 'to take the children's bread and throw it to the dogs.' The woman clears this last barrier not only with great skill but also with admirable hope and humility. 'Yes, Lord', she says, 'yet even the dogs eat the crumbs that fall from their master's table.' At this Jesus rewards her persistence: 'O woman, great is your faith! Be it done for you as you desire.'

Our Lord had placed four successive barriers in the way of the Canaanite woman's petition in order to raise her human hope to the height of a supernatural hope. At the same time he gave his apostles a salutary lesson.

3. *The multiplication of the loaves* (Mark vi, 34–44)

Here the tactics of Jesus before working a miracle consist in making the apostles measure the full extent of the problem, so that they may be fully convinced that there is no human solution for it.

Jesus has been speaking for a long time to the crowd who besiege him, so long indeed that the disciples feel they must intervene and make him listen to reason. 'This is a lonely place', they say, 'and the hour is now late; send them away, to go into the country and villages round about and buy themselves something to eat.' His reply is abrupt and disconcerting: 'You give them something to eat!'

John supplies an extra detail, for he says that Jesus addressed himself to Philip 'to test him, for he himself knew what he would do' (John vi, 6). And Philip, replying for the others, says somewhat vehemently: 'Two hundred denarii would not buy enough bread for each of them to get a little.' Two hundred denarii was an enormous sum at this time. A denarius was the daily wage of a worker (cf. the parable of the labourers in the vineyard).

This time Jesus makes them aware of a new dimension of their powerlessness by asking them to find out what resources the crowd has. Moreover, he orders them to make the multitude sit down in groups of hundreds and fifties so that they can be counted.

Jesus multiplies the loaves and fishes so abundantly that the remains fill twelve baskets.

The apostles have had an opportunity to gauge the full extent of their helplessness—all the factors make the problem insoluble. It is late, they are far away from all sources of supply, they have no money, they have almost no food, and the crowd is enormous. In short, the situation is hopeless. But what is not possible to resolve by human means will be more than sufficiently solved by a single word from Jesus. To Jesus, nothing is impossible.

4. *The Storm is calmed* (Matt. viii, 23–27; Mark iv, 35–40; Luke viii, 22–23)

Jesus gets into a boat with his disciples on the evening of a working day. A violent storm suddenly arises, as happens on lake Tiberias. The angry waves beat on the boat, almost swamping it, and endanger the lives of the men. Jesus is in the stern, fast asleep on a cushion. If he were awake, the disciples would not be afraid, but then their confidence would not be put to the test. Jesus is asleep and this makes them feel almost as if he is not there. His sleep may also be a lesson in confidence, but the sudden and serious danger makes the disciples impervious to such a lesson. Panic-stricken, they wake Jesus, asking him reproachfully: 'Teacher, do you not care if we perish?' which shows how they have lost their nerve. Jesus calms the storm and draws his lesson from the episode. 'Why are you afraid?' he asks them. 'Have you no faith?' This lesson was to impress the disciples, who were well used to the lake and its temper, and fully realized that they had narrowly escaped death. Now they were frightened, no longer by the storm, but by the power of Christ. And they continued to exchange their impressions in whispers until they had crossed the lake. They had just begun to discover that with Christ nothing was impossible.

5. *The raising of Lazarus* (John xi, 1-44)

Three times the evangelist emphasizes the affection Jesus had
for the family at Bethany, and especially for Lazarus. We can see
this in the case of Lazarus when his sisters speak to Jesus of him;
he is indicated to Jesus by his sisters with those expressive words:
'he whom you love.' And the evangelist adds: 'Now Jesus loved
Martha and her sister and Lazarus.' When Jesus weeps over the
body of Lazarus, the Jews say: 'See how he loved him!' This
affection makes Jesus' attitude even more astonishing. 'So when
he heard that he was ill, he stayed two days longer in the place
where he was.' To spare himself the urgent entreaties of his
disciples he speaks those reassuring words of which the meaning
only becomes clear at the end of the story: 'This illness is not
unto death; it is for the glory of God, so that the Son of God may
be glorified by means of it.'

After remaining where he was until Lazarus's illness ended in
death, Jesus at last decided to set out for Bethany, and he gave
a reason for his delay. 'Lazarus is dead', he tells his disciples, 'and
for your sake I am glad that I was not there, so that you may
believe.' The long distance to Bethany explains the fact that
Jesus and his disciples do not arrive until four days after the burial,
when the body is already beginning to decompose.

It is not only the apostles' hope that Jesus wishes to test, but
also that of Martha and Mary. His natural kindness has not
spared the two sisters the suffering caused by the death of their
brother. 'When the Jews who were with her in the house, con-
soling her, saw Mary rise quickly and go out, they followed her,
supposing that she was going to the tomb to weep there. Then
Mary, when she came where Jesus was and saw him, fell at his
feet, saying to him: "Lord, if you had been here, my brother
would not have died." When Jesus saw her weeping . . . he was
deeply moved.' He has the stone removed from the tomb, but
Martha, in her realistic way, remarks that after four days in the
tomb the body will be beginning to smell. And Jesus replies

emphatically: 'Did I not tell you that if you would believe you would see the glory of God?'

Jesus allowed events to develop without intervening, so that no one would have the slightest human hope left. He wished that all, the two sisters as well as his disciples, should confess their supernatural hope in his power. The words of Martha certainly express this hope: 'I believe that you are the Christ, the Son of God, he who is coming into the world.'

We could multiply examples of this patient teaching on the part of Jesus. It is a long training which is to end with the great lesson of his death and resurrection. Without this last lesson nothing of all they had learned would have lived on in the minds of the apostles. But for the Twelve the death of Jesus was the end of all the human hopes they had cherished of the restoration of the kingdom of Israel. And the resurrection of the Lord, although it had often been foretold by Jesus, was at first received with amazement and suspended belief.

But Jesus multiplied the most tangible proofs of the reality of his resurrection. He allowed the apostles to touch him and to feel his wounds, and he ate and drank with them, before ascending to his Father. The conviction that their Lord was alive, that he was seated for ever more at the right hand of the heavenly Father, was the basis of the apostles' hope, and also the binding force of their fidelity.

II. HOPE IN THE KINGDOM

At the same time that the apostles, in their response to Jesus, were to pass from human hope in the man Jesus to supernatural hope in the power of the Son of God, they were to traverse the same stages in their concept of the kingdom, and to pass from human to supernatural hope.

1. *What was the apostles' hope in the kingdom?*

The apostles shared the mentality of their contemporaries in their aspirations and in the ideas that moved them. The most intense of these ideas, and the most dynamic, too, was that of the kingdom of God.[1] It was the most profound mainspring, the very soul of the hope of Israel.

Its starting point was the covenant concluded between God and his chosen people. The Israelites had been repeatedly unfaithful to this covenant, and had been severely punished for their unfaithfulness. But God remained faithful, and his covenant with his people was final. The prophets had often affirmed this, and their words, built into the nation's memory, were a permanent source of great hope.

'For behold, I create new heavens and a new earth; and the former things shall not be remembered or come into mind. But be glad and rejoice for ever in that which I create; for behold, I create Jerusalem a rejoicing, and her people a joy' (Is. lxv, 17-19). 'For they shall be the offspring of the blessed of the Lord, and their children with them. Before they call I will answer, while they are yet speaking I will hear' (Is. lxv, 23-24). 'I will heal their faithlessness; I will love them freely, for my anger has turned from them. I will be as the dew to Israel; he shall blossom as the lily, he shall strike root as the poplar; his shoots shall spread out ...' (Hos. xiv, 4-6). 'I will restore the fortunes of my people Israel, and they shall rebuild the ruined cities and inhabit them ... I will plant them upon their land, and they shall never again be plucked up out of the land which I have given them, says the Lord your God' (Amos ix, 14-15). In short, the covenant which God concluded with his people overcomes Israel's unfaithfulness: God will have his hour, but Israel will not only be the instrument of the triumph but, more important, will benefit from it.

The Jews in the time of Jesus were living on these promises, and they cherished them all the more because they had been oppressed by successive conquerers for centuries, and were then

1. St Matthew always says: 'the kingdom of heaven'. The choice of the word 'heaven' stems, no doubt, from the Jewish habit of not uttering the name of God.

under the yoke of the Romans. We know, by comparison with recent history and current events, the depth and dynamism of these popular aspirations. The desire for political liberty, epitomized by the French Revolution, kept Europe in a ferment during the whole of the nineteenth century. The present thirst for national independence comes to complete the transformation of a whole continent colonized by Europe. The Jews were animated with Messianic yearnings, and everyone had his own ideas on the subject, according to his spiritual depth. All awaited a kingdom and all awaited a Messiah.

This kingdom that was to come, this future age, would have a religious and moral aspect: justice would reign, and each person would be rewarded according to his deserts, especially for the way he had fulfilled the essence of Jewish religion summed up in the Law of Moses. It would also have a material side which might be called 'triumphalist'; Israel would not only regain her liberty, but also subdue foreign nations.

As for the Messiah, he was the centre of these aspirations, and people's conceptions of what he would be dominated their different ideas of the kingdom of God. In the minds of some he was the liberator, the temporal saviour, the warrior king. In the minds of others he was also the spiritual saviour, the suffering servant of Yahweh, the suffering Messiah and redeemer (Is. liii, Ps. xxii).

At the dawn of the New Testament we see holy people awaiting the Messiah and the kingdom. The angel speaks to Mary in language she can understand: 'And the Lord God will give to him the throne of his father David, and he will reign over the house of Jacob for ever; and of his kingdom there will be no end' (Luke i, 32-33). On the birth of his son John the Baptist, Zechariah says: 'Blessed be the Lord God of Israel, for he has visited and redeemed his people . . . to remember his holy covenant, the oath which he swore to our father Abraham' (Luke i, 68-73). And Simeon is 'looking for the consolation of Israel' (Luke ii, 25).

The apostles are of the same race and the same *milieu*. But their hope is less pure than that of the persons we have just quoted. Its spiritual elements are freely mixed with 'carnal' ones, and all the educational efforts of Jesus are aimed at turning this human hope to supernatural hope.

2. *What is the hope to which Jesus wishes to lead his apostles?*

The kingdom of which he repeatedly speaks to them presents characteristics so paradoxical that the apostles find them hard to assimilate. It would have been simple for Jesus to say: 'I am the Messiah.' Instead, he silences the possessed people who proclaim him to be 'the Holy One of God', 'the Son of God', 'the Son of the Most High God' (Mark i, 24; iii, 11-12; v, 7). He forbids his disciples to make him known as the Messiah; he flees from the enthusiastic crowds; he takes care that his miracles are not divulged. The impatience of the apostles is quite understandable—'How long will you keep us in suspense? If you are the Christ, tell us plainly' (Mark viii, 30; ix, 9; John vi, 14-16; x, 24).

But this obscurity and the diversity of the traits which characterize the kingdom of which he speaks so often, have an educational meaning. Jesus is preparing his apostles little by little for a revelation which they could not bear all at once, and of which his death, resurrection and ascension will be a decisive stage. By keeping their minds alert, he obliges them to maintain an attitude of active enquiry. But we, who have the message in its entirety, can discern in the kingdom three characteristics which must always be considered together because they define one single, very simple reality: the kingdom is already realized, it is growing, and it is to come.

(a) *The kingdom is already realized*

The disciples of John the Baptist come to Jesus to ask if he is 'he who is to come'. Jesus does not give them a direct reply.

Instead, he invites them to draw their own conclusions from what they have seen. 'Go and tell John what you have seen and heard: the blind receive their sight, the lame walk, lepers are cleansed, and the deaf hear, the dead are raised up, the poor have good news preached to them.' By adding: 'And blessed is he who takes no offence at me' (Luke vii, 22-23), Jesus places himself in the centre of this revelation of the kingdom as already present.

On another occasion Jesus, reproaching the scribes for their bad faith when they accuse him of acting under the influence of the prince of demons, ends by saying: 'But if it is by the finger of God that I cast out demons, then the kingdom of God has come upon you' (Luke xi, 20).

But the messengers of John, and these scribes, and evidently the apostles, too, were expecting visible and striking signs of this coming of the kingdom. This is why Jesus says to them: 'The kingdom of God is not coming with signs to be observed; nor will they say. "Lo, here it is!" or "There!" for behold, the kingdom of God is in the midst of you' (Luke xvii, 20-21). This was yet another invitation to turn their minds towards Jesus himself.

(b) *The kingdom is growing*

The discourses of Jesus disconcert everybody. His own disciples question him; John the Baptist's disciples do not understand him; the masses, always easily roused, are just as easily disconcerted. We must bear in mind this lack of understanding when we read the parables which describe a growing kingdom, remembering that this method of teaching had to be suited to the audience which might be reserved or excitable. The parables of the sower, of the growing seed, of the tares in the wheat, and of the grain of mustard seed, must have been related by Jesus to explain both his own ministry and all future preaching of the Gospel. When we read the parables in their over-all context, and not in the progressive educational curriculum in which they were narrated, we find in them the mysticism and also the asceticism common to all forms of apostolate. Every single word is important, every single grain in the mysterious growth of the word which, like the grain itself, does not come to the fulness of life until it has passed through death ('unless a grain of wheat . . . dies'). We can see the need to open the heart when it receives the word as the earth receives seed; it can let it die, or suffocate it, or help it to increase. Of course, the word needs time to mature just as seed does, and the sower of the word cannot hasten its growth when the mystery of this growth and the time required for it elude him —'The kingdom of God is as if a man should scatter seed upon the ground, and should sleep and rise night and day, and the seed should sprout and grow, he knows not how' (Mark iv, 26–27). There is a fundamental disproportion between the feebleness of the word in its first expression and the immensity of the ultimate results; between the grain of mustard seed, 'the smallest of all seeds on earth', and 'the greatest of all shrubs'; or between the little measure of leaven and the dough it must leaven (Mark iv, 31–32; Matt. xiii, 33). In all this we are taught to accept humble and poor means, together with the paradoxical scale of values in the beatitudes, in preference to the means and values which the world holds in high esteem. One can even see the mixture of good and bad in the growing kingdom, like the weeds among the good grain in the ripening harvest (Matt. xiii, 24–30; 36–43).

We can describe the growth once more as a homogeneous reality; but Jesus takes time to instil the doctrine of this reality into the minds of his disciples. To impart this very fertile and complex notion of a kingdom expanding until the end of time, Jesus employed the methods of a teacher who respects the principles of a measured and progressive education.

(c) *The kingdom which is to come*

When our Lord speaks to his apostles of a kingdom to come and not of a kingdom already present or growing, he always means the perfect kingdom at the end of time that has to be 'entered' (Matt. v, 20; vii, 21; etc.) at all costs if one is to achieve one's destiny, and from which one risks being excluded.

This kingdom to come is somehow the end of that long growth of which we have just been speaking (the greatest of all shrubs or the net filled with fish), but it is also a new moment, a breakaway from the preceding era, a new coming of the Son of man to judge mankind, that is to say, to separate the good from the wicked, the just from the unjust (Matt. xxiv, 42, etc.).

We who know the message in its entirety must unite in one mental vision all the dimensions which seem not to fit. It is with the kingdom as with all the spiritual realities bound up with it: they are given to us today, they are growing, and we shall receive them in a new and transcendent way on the 'last day'.[1]

But this teaching, so utterly different from what the apostles had expected, had to be imparted to them by degrees if it was to bear fruit in time. Our Lord firmly insisted, however, on some key-points to which they could refer in time of darkness.

3. *The absolute value of the kingdom of God*

This kingdom is in fact an absolute value, besides which nothing else counts or has the slightest value. 'The kingdom of heaven is like *treasure* hidden in a field, which a man found and covered up; then *in his joy* he goes and sells *all that he has* and buys that field. Again the kingdom of heaven is like a merchant in search of fine pearls, who, on finding *one pearl of great value,* went and sold *all* that he had and bought it' (Matt. xiii, 44-46).

Nothing in the world, either in the order of values or in the material order, can compare with the kingdom, the value of which is transcendent. It is definitely not something to which we can give a discreetly limited place in our life: we cannot possess

1. The Liturgy itself accustoms us to live in the three dimensions. See, for instance, the hymn for matins in Advent: '*Verbum supernum prodiens e Patris aeterni sinu, qui natus orbi subvenis labente cursu temporis. Illumina nunc pectora . . . ut cum tribunal Judicis . . . etc.*'

the kingdom until everything else has been abandoned for it. It was Newman who said: 'Ask yourself if, in the event of the kingdom having disappeared, you would have had to change something in your life. If you see nothing to change, this means that you have not staked your life on Christ and his kingdom.'

All the reflections ever made, down the ages, on the absolute nature of the kingdom are contained in embryo in the parables of the hidden treasure and the pearl of great price. But for the disciples hearing them for the first time, they are the start of a slow germination which gradually takes place in their minds as their time with Jesus passes.

How far all this is from the calculations of human ambition, even when the latter is concealed beheath a pseudo-religious ideal! The apostles cannot attain to a pure vision of the kingdom to which they are called. They have left all to follow Christ, but they definitely hope to be ministers of the kingdom they are to help to establish. It is from this psychological perspective that we must understand the plea of the mother of James and John (Matt. xx, 20-23) and the last request of the apostles at the moment of the ascension (Acts i, 6).

But Jesus calls them constantly back to the essential by opening their eyes to the spiritual conditions needed for entry into the kingdom. It is not enough to be a member, nor even to have made a certain choice, nor to collaborate willingly like someone who invests a sum of money at a good interest. All such things belong to the domain of human hope, but have nothing in common with theological hope.

One who has chosen the kingdom leaves 'the dead to bury their own dead' (Matt. viii, 22), makes his arrangements ahead to avoid having to reconsider his undertaking in the course of his work or journey (Luke xiv, 28-33), and cannot love his father, his mother, his son or his daughter more than the Lord (Matt. x, 37). He has to be in a constant state of spiritual conversion, and capable of self-examination (Luke v, 31; Matt. ix, 13; Luke xviii,

4-19, etc.), because Jesus has only come to call those who know themselves sinners. We could give many more instances, but here it is enough to say that what is required is integral Christianity—a life lived according to the Gospels. Here we have the complete antithesis of the kingdom the apostles expected and for which they were following Christ. It is in another world; it is a kingdom of another order, of which all the values are paradoxical, where the role of human hope cannot be seen, and where there is no place for either worldly ambition or half-measures.

4. *The bond between the kingdom and Christ*

To choose the kingdom means to choose Christ. This affirmation seems self-evident, but if we reflect a little we shall discover a new light on the education given by Jesus to his apostles, and the deep meditation it merits.

After finding the Messiah, the disciples had followed him with true devotion. They could not dedicate themselves to the restoration of the kingdom of Israel without throwing in their lot with him who was to be its head. In human history those who have put their faith in a movement of liberation or conquest under a leader have always had to throw in their lot with him, for better or for worse. But our Lord is to overthrow this all too human scale of values in which the interest of the kingdom has so much more weight than the person of the leader. Jesus wishes his apostles to stake their whole lives on him personally, without compensation, without consolation, and at the risk of all they have.

We shall speak of this at greater length in the following chapter, but we would merely emphasize the aim here. It is not a matter of choosing a life, noble though that may be; it is a matter of *choosing a person*, of attaching ourselves to him without calculation; of putting him before all human affections, even the deepest. Whether it is a matter of the kingdom already present, or of the growing kingdom, or of the kingdom to come, the person of Jesus always intervenes as summing-up the very riches of the kingdom and all the motives for commitment to it.

To ensure that there should be no misunderstanding in the minds of the apostles, and that their choice should be at once fully enlightened and completely disinterested, Jesus does not hesitate to emphasize the painful aspect of his mission. It is in this spirit that we should reread the Gospel story of the passion and the progressively clearer prophecies of it.

If the apostles wish to restore the kingdom of Israel, they must put Christ in first place, and love him above all else. And in order that their choice may be disinterested, or at least lean in this direction, the perspective of the passion of Jesus has to be engraved in their vision of the future. When the mother of James and John demands that her sons have the highest offices in the future kingdom, Jesus says to the ambitious young men: 'You do not know what you are asking. Are you able to drink the cup that I am to drink?' (Matt. xx, 20-22).

And more than once Jesus announces his future sufferings to the apostles. No doubt he often prophesies the passion and resurrection as two inseparable stages of the one unique mystery. But it is certainly with the servant of the Lord, the suffering servant of Isaiah's prophecy (Is. liii), that he identifies himself (Luke xiii, 31-33; Matt, xxiii, 19-32; Mark ix, 12; Luke xvii, 25; Matt. xvi, 21; xvii, 22-23; xx, 18-19).

To show this, let us simply return to his reply to James and John. Having asked them: 'Are you able to drink the cup that I am to drink?', he comments on the incident to all the apostles, and ends his reprimand with these words: 'The Son of man came not to be served but *to serve and to give his life as a ransom for many*' (Matt. xx, 28). Is not this precisely the mission of the 'servant of Yahweh' who was 'wounded for our transgressions' (Is. liii, 5), and who makes 'many to be accounted righteous' by his sufferings (Is. liii, 11)?

Some days later, on the eve of his passion, when Jesus eats the

Last Supper with his apostles and institutes the eucharist, he says: 'For I tell you that from now on I shall not drink of the fruit of the vine until the kingdom of God comes' (Luke xxii, 18). He will drink with them 'when I drink it new with you in my Father's kingdom' (Matt. xxvi, 29). He tells his disciples that he is leaving them, but it is in order to accomplish the kingdom announced from the time of his coming on earth.

Much more research and a much lengthier study would be needed to describe adequately the patient education that Jesus gave his apostles in order to make them change from hope in an earthly kingdom and an earthly messiah to hope in the kingdom of heaven and in the Lord who died and rose again.

As it happens, this education is one long succession of disappointments for those who receive it, and even on the morning of the ascension they ask again: 'Lord, will you at this time restore the kingdom of Israel?' (Acts i, 6).

The Holy Spirit is to continue this work during the rest of the apostles' lives. Jesus promises them this: 'But you shall receive power when the Holy Spirit has come upon you; and you shall be my witnesses . . . to the end of the earth' (Acts i, 8).

After the ascension of our Lord, the apostles received the promise of his return: 'This Jesus, who was taken up from you into heaven, will come in the same way as you saw him go into heaven' (Acts i, 11). Henceforward they believed in the return of Jesus: they longed for him ardently, and in the beginning they certainly expected an early return. In this also they had to experience a disappointment in order that their hope might be purified. Christ did not come back as they expected. But their hope, pressing ahead, made them more capable of seeing that the kingdom of God was growing before the eyes of their faith and that the Lord was still living with them, in his Church.

14

Jesus Trains the Apostles in Faithfulness

WE have seen that being faithful consists in adhering to God so earnestly that eventually we renounce ourselves, together with all our fixed earthly ideas, our own scale of values, our warped love, in order to enter into God's plan and perspective and to tend towards faithfulness in him.

But this faithfulness is not acquired all at once. Not only is it a grace from God, but it is a grace given throughout a whole life. It involves sufferings, crosses, defeats, and the monotony of time. It demands that we cling resolutely to God alone when our strength is at breaking-point, when suffering seems to be a senseless denial of God's fatherly kindness and defeat a denial of his power. And yet how could our faithfulness be proved if the conflict brought by circumstances did not constantly test and fortify our inner resources?

It is true that God reserves particularly painful trials for his friends. Otherwise how would they know the quality and strength of their love? Love does not really become strong as death until it has survived this daily death by trials, until it no longer clings to God except by the fine point of the will, when all else seems lost.

The apostles experienced this, not only while Jesus was with them, but also after his ascension. They tried to follow this path of faithfulness all their lives, for it is a path that has no end. Throughout their life with Jesus he was their master, and an exacting master, as we shall see. After pentecost the Holy Spirit was their guide, as he is the guide of all those whom Christ calls to the life of faith today.

But although our Lord was exacting yet he knew how to

regulate trials, and he was with his disciples to reveal their meaning to them. When he called Peter, he did not say to him: 'Follow me, and you will be crucified head downwards.' He said to him and the others: 'Follow me, and I will make you fishers of men' (Matt. iv, 21). And even when he left him at the ascension, after entrusting him with the feeding of his sheep, he only foretold his future fate in veiled terms: 'Truly, truly, I say to you, when you were young, you girded yourself and walked where you would; but when you are old, you will stretch out your hands, and another will gird you and carry you where you do not wish to go' (John xxi, 18). The evangelist who relates this last prophecy of Jesus survived Peter long enough to understand its meaning and to add: 'This he said to show by what death he was to glorify God' (John xxi, 19).

When the apostles first met Jesus, for some it was by the banks of the Jordan, for some at Capernaum or on the shores of lake Tiberias. They were won over at the very first meeting and followed his call, but they did not know at the time all the consequences of that first decision to follow. The work of a long apostolic life, and for most of them ultimate martyrdom—in short, their exemplary faithfulness—all was included in that first 'yes'. But they did not know it, and were to discover it only slowly at the cost of much patience and many defeats. All was there in embryo in that first 'yes', but it had to grow.

If we read the Gospels and the Acts of the Apostles we can follow the apostles' progress in faithfulness through all the trials to which Jesus subjected them. And the epistles of St Paul, St Peter and St John enable us to follow the later stages of this growth under the action of the Holy Spirit.

At first sight, when we try to picture the progress of faithfulness, we imagine it as a regular and gentle growth, like a night which gradually changes to dawn, then to full day, and finally to bright sunshine. But in reality the example of the apostles shows us that fidelity emerges from a succession of infidelities; it results from many disappointments, defeats and crises, provided that these are overcome. This is what the apostles experienced until the tragedy of Calvary and even until the break brought about by the ascension, which marks the final collapse of their hopes for the restoration of the kingdom of Israel.

The apostles grew in fidelity as they discovered by experience the mystery of the death and resurrection of Jesus. And it was the Holy Spirit who was to make them understand clearly the things Jesus had said to show them the way. 'If any man would come after me, let him deny himself and take up his cross daily and follow me ... Whoever loses his life for my sake, he will save it' (Luke ix, 23-24). 'Was it not necessary that the Christ should suffer these things and enter into his glory' (Luke xxiv, 26).

As we have done above, we shall search the Gospels to see the means by which our Lord tried and welded anew the fidelity of the apostles.

1. *Christ drives the traders and money-changers from the Temple* (John ii, 13)

The evangelist St John relates his memories of the first days of his life with Jesus. The smallest details have remained graven in his memory, and as he puts them down in writing in the evening of his life, he sees their providential range and bearing. He tells of Jesus' first disciples—his calling of Andrew, Simon, Philip and Nathanael. Three days after this, accompanied by these first five followers, Jesus attends a marriage feast at Cana in Galilee and changes water into wine. John says Jesus 'manifested his glory; and his disciples believed in him' (ii, 11). The seed of faith is thus sown in their hearts. But we may well wonder what this Jesus they believe in means to them. No doubt they regard him as the Messiah, but one invested with a nimbus of earthly hopes for the restoration of the kingdom of Israel. Today they are the first companions, and tomorrow they will be the ministers of a leader who will liberate their country. Jesus is to shatter these ambitions by inflicting a first trial on them. In fact, a few days after the miracle of Cana he goes up to Jerusalem for the passover. There he drives the traders from the Temple and provokes such a public disturbance that the authorities have to intervene. To their questions, Jesus replies in an apparently off-hand manner: 'Destroy this temple, and in three days I will raise it up' (John ii, 19). Obviously the disciples did not understand, for St John tells us clearly that these words had no meaning for them until after the resurrection of their Lord. Let us put ourselves in the apostles' place: they must have thought that Jesus was setting about the inauguration of his mission rather badly, and that they had probably entered on a foolish venture. But they stood firm.

2. *The discourse on the bread of life* (John vi, 22–70)

A year passed. The miracles of Jesus multiplied and the crowds who followed him became more and more enthusiastic. One evening they remained so long listening to him up in the hills with nothing to eat that Jesus had to multiply loaves and fishes to feed them. The people became wildly excited at this, and suddenly some of them took it into their heads to carry off Jesus and make him king. We do not know whether the apostles were aware of this plan or not. At any rate, Jesus slipped away from the crowd and from the apostles and took refuge in a solitary place.

When he rejoined the disciples and the crowd in the synagogue at Capernaum, he tried to quell their natural enthusiasm and gave the discourse on the bread of life, in which we see so clearly how he tried the faith of his disciples and what painful reactions this particular discourse provoked.

Right at the start the crowd began to turn against him. 'The Jews then murmured at him, because he said. "I am the bread which came down from heaven." They said: "Is not this Jesus, the son of Joseph, whose father and mother we know?" ' A little later the crowd showed their lack of understanding again. 'How can this man give us his flesh to eat?' they asked. In short, the whole discourse on the bread of life ended in general hostility, and the contrast between the enthusiasm of the previous evening after the multiplication of the loaves and fishes and the violent reaction towards this obviously displeasing discourse, is very remarkable. The disciples felt this contrast all the more since the words of Jesus were as puzzling for them as for the crowd. Their fidelity to Jesus and their faith in him were completely shaken once more. 'Many of his disciples, when they heard it, said, "This is a hard saying; who can listen to it?" ' At this moment Jesus could have done what he had done in other circumstances: he could have explained the obscure discourse aside to his disciples. But without any effort to smooth over the difficulty he asked them baldly: 'Do you take offence at this? Then what if you were to see the Son of man ascending where he was before?' This prediction of the Easter mystery only added one obscurity to another. And Jesus added sternly: 'But there are some of you that do not believe.'

The challenge had such an effect that many of his disciples renounced their fidelity, which was costing them too much when it ran counter to all good sense, and to the security they needed in the small designs of their narrow lives. 'After this many of his disciples drew back and no longer went about with him.'

A handful remained—the Twelve—and Jesus knew that there was a traitor among these and that others were wavering. One might think that our Lord would have felt he had tried them enough, and would have relieved the anxiety of the apostles, restoring their shaken faith with some kind words. But to strengthen fidelity by kind words is not God's way, and he tested them to the end. In giving them their liberty, Jesus drove home the point: 'Will you also go away?' he asked. It was then that Simon Peter, in the midst of his puzzlement, reaffirmed his fidelity: 'Lord, to whom shall we go? You have the words of eternal life; and we have believed and have come to know, that you are the holy one of God.' And Jesus ended the interview with the stern words: 'Did I not choose you, the Twelve, and one of you is a devil?'

This test only partially destroyed the apostles' all too human ideas about the mission of Jesus, but it increased their faithfulness. For faithfulness only grows when we are free of ideas which are too human, and accept God's mysterious plan without question. This detachment and this acceptance are not the fruit of intellectual reflections; they are only achieved after a great trial, when a person remains firm.

3. *Peter's confession of faith and the first prophecy of the passion* (Matt. xvi, 13-25)

One day Jesus questioned his apostles about himself. 'Who do men say that the Son of man is?' he asked them. On receiving some hesitant replies he continued his questioning in a more pointed way: 'But who do *you* say that I am?' Peter replied: 'You are the Christ, the Son of the living God.' Jesus thereupon praised him openly, saying that he had been inspired by the heavenly Father. Then he added: 'And I tell you, you are Peter, and on this rock I will build my church . . . I will give you the keys of the kingdom of heaven . . .'

A vital stage had been reached that day, for this was the first act of explicit faith in the messianic character of Jesus. But Jesus forbade his disciples to tell anyone that he was the Christ.

The apostles' faith, confirmed anew, was not allowed to expand in peace. Before they had recovered from the shock of their last trial of faith, Jesus explicitly announced his coming passion. 'From that time Jesus began to show his disciples that he must go to Jerusalem and suffer many things from the elders and chief priests and scribes, and be killed, and on the third day be raised.'

Peter, still greatly excited by the revelations made to him and the compliment Jesus had paid him, felt bold enough to rebuke his Lord and induce him to take a less pessimistic view of things. 'God forbid, Lord!' he exclaimed. 'This shall never happen to you!' But with a brusqueness that contrasted painfully with the warmth of his recent words, Jesus replied: 'Get behind me, Satan! you are a hindrance to me; for you are not on the side of God, but of men.' This was precisely what Peter had still to lose—the human way of thinking that dominated his mind in spite of himself—if he was to adopt once and for all the thoughts of God. And this is why he was to be tried still more.

4. *The transfiguration and the second prophecy of the passion* (Mark ix, 2-13)

Peter, James and John were chosen by Jesus to be witnesses of the transfiguration. They saw the glory of Jesus and they heard the words of his heavenly Father: 'This is my beloved Son; listen to him.' And immediately Jesus announced to them again that he would 'suffer many things and be treated with contempt' before rising from the dead. Once more, trial followed consolation, putting their fidelity to the test. But meanwhile the consolation enabled them to bear the trial, of which they would one day reap the fruit.

5. *The raising of Lazarus and another prophecy of the passion* (John xi; xii, 7)

The raising of Lazarus had been another amazing event for the apostles. But after the supper given in his honour by Lazarus and his sisters, Jesus took the opportunity when Mary anointed him with precious ointment to speak of his burial (John xii, 7). He always followed the same method which he was soon to express in a striking formula that is a clue to the mystery of the trials God sends his servants. 'I am the true vine', he said, 'and my Father is the vinedresser . . . every branch that does bear fruit he prunes, that it may bear more fruit' (John xv, 1-2). We cannot progress in fidelity unless we are 'pruned' by the heavenly Father.

6. *The death of Jesus tests the apostles' fidelity*

The triumph of Palm Sunday had renewed the apostles' hope.

After so many vicissitudes, it made the restoration of the kingdom of Israel through Jesus, the descendant of David, seem nearer than ever before. But now the drama of the passion suddenly looms up. Certainly, the Twelve had not been indifferent to the suffering of their Lord. But it is not his suffering that occupies their conscious minds. These are filled with the confusion and amazement produced by what seems to them the radical and final defeat of Jesus, the absolute destruction of all their dreams, the collapse of all their human hopes. It is their own drama, not the drama of Jesus that overwhelms them. We can see this from their psychological inability to accompany Jesus in his agony, and in the ease with which Peter denies his Lord; and all the apostles abandon him to the Jews.

We cannot say they lacked faith. They had believed in Jesus. Peter's tone of conviction when he declared: 'You are the Christ' (Matt. xvi, 16) was not feigned, nor was that of Thomas: 'Let us also go, that we may die with him' (John xi, 16). But this fidelity was weighed down with human elements, personal desires, worldly ambitions (Matt. xx, 20-23). Their attachment to Jesus was serious and sincere, but their thoughts were not God's thoughts, and they could not rise to his level by any ordinary psychological effort. Jesus had often foretold his surrender and death; they heard but they did not understand. That was why their fidelity had to be tried; the vine-branch had to be pruned by the Father. The passion of Jesus was to be the final test of their fidelity. Jesus was to say: 'Simon, Simon, behold, Satan demanded to have you, that he might sift you like wheat' (Luke xxii, 31). And again: 'You will all fall away; for it is written, "I will strike the shepherd, and the sheep will be scattered" ' (Mark xiv, 27). They could say later, as the disciples on the way to Emmaus were to say, 'We had hoped' (Luke xxiv, 21). They had hoped, on the merely human level, that the Messiah would place himself at the head of his people and vanquish the Romans. But, as it was, the chiefs of the people had become the accomplices of the Romans in order to deliver Jesus up to them, and the people had sanctioned this treachery by shouting for his death. How could they still believe that Jesus, who had been rejected by the people, mocked and crucified as a common malefactor, and abandoned by God, and who has finally died on the cross, could be the Messiah?

For a long time Judas had inwardly abandoned the party, for his fidelity had been too severely tried. But how about the others? What painful renunciation was being asked of them? They were in complete darkness. Abandoning their families to follow Christ was nothing compared to what was being asked of them now; for they were being asked to strip themselves of their mentality. One can abandon one's family freely by a final act of will, whereas one's mentality clings to one's inmost being, and only suffering can effect this forcible detachment. And the very word 'detachment' is not strong enough to express what the apostles were to undergo. It was rather a 'stripping bare'.

But the apostles had not lost their love for our Lord. The proof of this was that on Easter Sunday they had gathered together once more to honour his memory. But it was the memory of a dead man they were honouring, and this reunion was meant as a preparation for their dispersion and return to their former occupations. Two of the disciples had already set out for Emmaus. The predictions of his death and resurrection which Jesus had so often made had been listened to, but neither understood nor remembered. The shock of events had shattered everything. They could not understand that the killing of Jesus could be part of God's plan. Their fidelity had to pass the test of blood, the blood of Jesus and the blood of their own hearts. While waiting for the risen Christ to come and take them by the hand and lead them out of it, they were submerged in a night of the darkest despair, and their fidelity hung on a thread.

7. The trial of Christ's ascension

Even when Jesus vanquished death by his resurrection, this

was not enough to change the mental outlook of the apostles, for on the very morning of the ascension they asked him: 'Lord, will you at this time restore the kingdom of Israel?' (Acts i, 6). Human standards were so much a part of them that the apostles could only be freed from these when Christ deprived them of his visible presence at the time of his ascension into heaven.

Hence we can understand Jesus telling them: 'It is good for you that I go away' (John xvi, 7). This was the price of the apostles' fidelity. One cannot help recalling how Yahweh forbade his chosen people to represent him in the form of images (Ex. xxxiv, 17; the molten calf, Ex. xxxii). In both cases it is an education in fidelity accomplished by removal of all sensible presence. In one of his sermons St Leo the Great tells how our Lord's ascension strengthened the apostles' faith:

'The ascension of the Lord, he says, was so profitable to the apostles . . . that all the contemplative activity of their souls henceforth turned to the divinity of him who is seated at the right hand of the Father. The sight of his person no longer hindered their minds from considering this mystery: that in coming down from heaven Christ did not separate himself from his Father any more than in ascending thence he separated himself from his disciples. The Son of God began in an ineffable manner to be present in his divinity the more he withdrew himself in his humanity. It was from the time of the ascension that faith, better instructed, learned to rise by a spiritual ascent to the Son of God equal to the Father, and no longer needed to touch in Christ that body by which he is inferior to the Father . . . The faith of believers has been raised to where the only begotten Son, equal to the Father, can no longer be reached by human hand, but only by the spiritual intelligence.'[1]

And so we see how this last stage of the apostles' growth in

1. St Leo the Great, *2nd Homily on the Ascension of the Lord.*

fidelity was also formed by a previous 'stripping' which was clearly most painful. Their love of Jesus was something that mattered supremely to the apostles. Peter had said to him shortly before: 'Lord, you know everything; you know that I love you' (John xxi, 17). Is not love always nurtured by the sensible presence of the beloved? Not necessarily; or at least, not when it is the kind of love identical with fidelity, and this is what God expects. Then it is not real presence but real absence that best nurtures it. 'It is good for you that I go away.' Here, sensible absence is replaced by presence by faith. Fidelity, therefore, is the true name of that love which God expects of us. And it neither exists nor deepens unless we achieve detachment, and strengthen our souls by endless self-denial.

Conclusion

IN the foregoing pages (Part IV) we have only tried to describe how Jesus carried out the training in faith of his apostles. When he left them, this training was still unfinished, not only because the growth of faith lasts a whole lifetime but also because Jesus had promised to send them another teacher, the paraclete, the Holy Spirit, to continue this education.

We can perceive throughout the epistles how the apostles were united to Jesus with every fibre of their being. Certain texts have a profoundly moving tone. St John, for instance, says: 'That which . . . we have heard, which we have seen with our eyes, which we have looked upon and touched with our hands, concerning the word of life . . . that which we have seen and heard we proclaim also to you . . . that our joy may be complete' (1 John i, 1-4); 'By this we know love, that he laid down his life for us' (1 John iii, 16). St Peter says: 'Without having seen him you love him; though you do not now see him you believe in him and rejoice with unutterable and exalted joy' (1 Peter i, 8).

In St Paul, texts like this are so numerous that here it is enough to quote one of them: 'Who shall separate us from the love of Christ? Shall tribulations, or distress, or persecution . . .?' (Rom. viii, 35).

But what far surpasses the most eloquent words is the witness of the apostles' lives and deaths. This witness was strong and fruitful enough for the faith of many generations to take root in it and grow in its turn. For faith engenders faith.

V

The Education and the Growth in Faith of the Christian of Today

> '*The greatest obstacle to progress in faith is not wickedness but complacency.*'
>
> Gabriel Marcel

Introduction

A STUDY such as this is only of interest if it throws light on the condition of the Christian of today. God called Abraham and Mary; he calls us also to a similar destiny and in doing so follows a similar plan.

Jesus formed his apostles in faith and he continues to give the same education, by his Holy Spirit, to those who allow themselves to be taught.

The response of Abraham or Mary, the faith of the apostles in Jesus, were all deeply marked by the age in which they lived, the needs of the generation to which they belonged. And our knowledge of their faith has been deepened by the meditation of the generations that have followed. It is the same today. God calls us personally by name. He calls us not only for our own good and profit, but also for the good of our generation and of the generations to come.

Just as the faith of Abraham has been the inspiration and support of all who have followed him, the faith of Mary a light to all those whom her son entrusted to her from the cross, and the faith of the apostles the foundation on which the Church was built, so too the faith of each one of us is given us that we may implant Christ and his Church in the world of the twentieth century, for today and for the future.

What is the situation that confronts us today? What is the task to which we are called? Let us look carefully at the contemporary situation and see the call of God that it conveys to us.

No thinking Christian can fail to be struck by the paganism, or rather the atheism, of the world in which we live. More and more books are analysing this phenomenon, and trying to find an answer.[1]

The faith of the Christian of today is both like that of his ancestors, and yet different. It is like it because it is a matter of adherence to the same Lord, with the same force and the same total commitment. It is different because this faith has to bear witness or 'pose a question' to the unbelievers of our time, in order that they too may dedicate their hearts and lives to the Lord.

What, then, are the problems which face the faith of the Christian of today?

1. The first thing that strikes us is the *massive character of the prevalent unbelief*. For modern unbelief presents itself in the form of a well systematized doctrine, whereas the unbelief of former times only existed in a more or less dispersed state, and no effort was made to justify it. Now there is a well-defined 'doctrine' of atheism consisting of several schools of thought—a Marxist atheism, and an existentialist atheism, for instance, the latter varying in different schools (those of Jean-Paul Sartre or Albert Camus, for example).

It is a matter of much more than simple paganism. Paganism has a real religiosity, and the multifarious gods which it accepts bear witness to a hidden nostalgia for the true God, whereas the atheism of today makes a clean sweep of every idea of God, and justifies his attitude by a complete system of unbelief. In fact, he seeks to propagate his atheism, which could more correctly be called a doctrinal and dynamic antitheism.

This is not the place to enlarge upon these established views, which are becoming commonplace. Our point is to show that,

1. Here are a few works, some of them very recent, which deal with this question:

Lubac, Henri du, S. J., *The Drama of Atheistic Humanism* (London, 1949)

Borne, E., *Modern Atheism* (London, 1961)

Rahner, Karl, S. J., *Mission and Grace* (London, 1963)

Marty, E. M., *Varieties of Unbelief* (New York, 1964)

Gleason, R. W., S. J., *The Search for God* (New York, 1964) faced with this world-wide atheism, the Christian must look into himself to discover the deep sources of his faith, nurture it and reinforce it so that it may become strong enough to bear witness.

Our faith is based on the certitude that God speaks and calls. Hence our first concern must be to know the word of God and to feed our souls on it; to realize that this word, though given centuries ago, is addressed personally to each one of us today. We must be full of pride in our faith, yet full of humility before its message; and full of such love for our fellows that we long to pass the good news on to them.

We have received the faith only to pass it on. But here again it must be deep and living, because faith cannot be passed on like words of wisdom, or like recipes. It is a flame that rises up from the depths of one heart to set other hearts alight. That is why the example of Abraham, Mary and the apostles has a topical value for us. They, too, found themselves in a pagan world, but their faith was dynamic enough to communicate itself to others.

The atheism of the world is a challenge flung at the Christian of today.

2. Our age is also marked by what has been called the *disappearance of 'Christendom'*. The process has been under way a very long time and it has been analysed again and again. Formerly the people of the West were born, lived and died in a Christian atmosphere. The family, the parish, civic life, the trades and professions, were all based on Christian ideas. The Church was present all through life. Human institutions were in effect an extension of her action. The schools were Christian; so were the hospitals. From the beginning of the renaissance men began to question this homogeneous civilization. It received a decisive shaking at the French Revolution. By defending the secular institutions the Church in France tried desperately to save this Christian social system, which was, in her eyes, one of the privileged vehicles of the faith. The history of the nineteenth and twentieth centuries might be epitomized as the history of

this struggle in the political, academic, social and charitable spheres. Only a few Christian institutions have survived up to the present, and these are more often than not almost submerged among secular institutions.

It must be admitted, then, that Christian civilization has been replaced by a secular or non-religious civilization. Christian institutions, academic and social, have been replaced by secular ones. As for Christian habits, they have long been disappearing little by little from the fabric of society.

The question arises: is the strength and expansion of the faith bound up with a given civilization and its institutions?

The present situation, which is the subject of so much lamenting, certainly obliges the Christian to deepen his faith and the knowledge of his religion, and this obligation is at once a call and a grace of God. Father Congar writes:

'When one looks at religious movements as a whole over the last hundred or hundred and thirty years, one can only see them as a reconquest and progressive restoration of Christianity on the ruins of the old Christian society which was overthrown by the ideological, political, economic and social revolution at the end of the eighteenth and beginning of the nineteenth century . . . It was a restoration of its whole vitality, a rediscovery of what is specifically Christian, a rediscovery even of the faith itself, in a world which has become more and more secularized. And the more the world becomes secularized and even returns to a kind of paganism, the more Christians have recourse to faith.'

We have not yet seen all the factors involved, but one thing certain is that the Christian, exposed to the cold blast of a pagan world, without the support of the warm and cosy atmosphere which his ancestors found in Christianity, is obliged to adapt his faith to the rigours of the climate, and consequently to train himself to a proportionate strength. The Christian is alone in the

face of the world. If his faith is not strong enough, his Christianity
will be swept away. Karl Rahner has called the present situation
of the Christian a '*diaspora*':

> 'The Church,' he says, 'is becoming a Church of the *diaspora*
> everywhere; a Church which lives dispersed among multitudes
> of non-Christians; a Church which has to inscribe its message in
> a cultural, civic, political, scientific and artistic context . . .
> which is not the work of Christians alone.'[1]

And Rahner goes on to show that when a Christian has to live
his faith in a predominantly non-Christian environment, this has
a number of immediate consequences. In the first place, his faith
is constantly threatened from without, and he must make a
reconquest of it 'in an environment full of danger'. Secondly, the
riches of culture upon which the Christian lives and must live are
no longer specifically Christian. Finally, it will no longer be
possible for the Church of the *diaspora* to be other than a Church
of active members, a Church of lay people convinced that they
have a real and active part in the Church and are not merely the
object of the clergy's pastoral care. It follows, then, that in this
situation of *diaspora* the Church will have a more directly religious aspect than formerly, and will turn inwards, of her own
will, to the very core of her being. She will be obliged to take off
a merely human garb in order to manifest her character as a
supernatural society. Instead of being a worldly power she will
become more and more the evangelical conscience of the world.

We should not be surprised at the diminished number of
Christians when 'Christendom' completely collapses. Formerly
everyone, or nearly everyone, was baptized and received the
other sacraments, and many 'practised' their religion. But the
number of the unbaptized is growing apace, and very often
nowadays the priest has to question the parents of the child he is

1. Karl Rahner, *Mission and Grace* (London, 1963), p. 43.

baptizing as to their faith, for they are meant to guarantee the future religious upbringing of the child.

As for 'religious practice', the many censuses being carried out on increasingly scientific lines show conclusively that it is steadily diminishing. There is nothing surprising in this. Here again, the position of Christians struggling against the cold wind of a secularized world is too trying for those of feeble faith.

We must remember, moreover, that the massive demographic changes of the present day are more favourable to non-Christian and neo-pagan peoples than to Christian populations. Hence it is certain that the quantitative decrease of Christians is the more striking in view of the numerical increase of the non-baptized.

When we consider the missionary responsibility of Christians at the present time in face of the multitudes of pagans whom they are meant to evangelize, we are painfully struck by the harmful witness which many Christians bear. Actually, they are Christians only in name, but pagan in their lives and actions. The prevalent atheism has penetrated their mentality, and it conditions their attitudes. It is a matter of convenience to distinguish between baptized and non-baptized, baptism being an objective, easily perceptible criterion, and the habit of using this criterion explains why many pastoral problems are badly stated today. In fact, we should distinguish between those who are in fact atheists, whether or not they are baptized or even 'practising', and Christians living their faith. Encumbered with moribund Christians, the Church cannot attain to her vital missionary dimensions. Many persons are atheists because they do not like the image of God which Christians present to them. They do not want 'the God of those people'. As long as there is such discrepancy between their religion (or religious practice) and their lives it will be impossible for Christians to evangelize the pagans around them at home. A return to the essential values of the Gospel is the only suitable response to the atheism of the masses. We must constantly ask ourselves: is the God whom the atheists of my acquaintance reject the living God, the God revealed by the prophets and by Jesus Christ? For the question concerns all of us personally. It is not a matter of examining other people's consciences, but our own. As Father Congar says:

'In each one of us there is a pagan, a Pharisee, and a Christian. The Christian life here below consists not so much in being Christian, as in trying, as far as we can, to become Christian.'

However, parallel with the decrease in numbers of which we have spoken earlier, we see an improvement in the quality of the *élite* who under the action of the Holy Spirit discover the necessity not only of deepening their faith, but of living in it all the dimensions of personal life and also of the life of the world. It is only in these conditions that a witness can exist, and experience proves that this witness is beginning to be given. The missionary spirit always begins by a transformation in depth.

3. In our time, the visible signs of the Church are changing. The Church is a mystery, but this mystery is presented to man by means of visible signs. Yesterday these visible signs were parishes. Today, it must be recognized that the greater number of parishes have ceased to be living communities either because they are excessively overgrown in urban areas, or depopulated in rural areas. Or more often, it is because they consist largely of Christians who habitually limit their commitment to the faith to mere practice, and have therefore ceased to be living communities. Consequently, they cannot be missionaries, nor can they even welcome converts. How many people we know who, converted to Christ, look in vain in Catholic parishes for a perceptible sign of a maternal Church!

However, here also a revival is already under way thanks to the impetus of pioneer priests and the demand of convinced Christians, who feel the importance of the parish community as a visible sign both for their own spiritual life and for the evangelization of non-Christians.

Furthermore, the organization of the pastoral ministry with a view to meeting social problems is steadily creating new and visible signs of a Church essentially missionary in outlook. In short, modern life, organized on rather socialist lines, more and more stratified in its social layers, and marked by an ever more mobile labour force, is bringing about new forms of life and relationships, in which the Church should be present.

This is why new types of Christian communities are springing up almost everywhere (Catholic Action teams, family groups, spiritual study groups, etc.), all of them vital in spreading the faith. The convinced Christians who form them become more and more aware, as their own faith deepens, that they are sons of the heavenly Father through Jesus Christ, and that consequently there is a vital need for human brotherhood.

The deeper realization of the meaning of the Church today is the result of a deepening of the faith in the hearts of many Christians. Certainly one of the most fruitful insights of Pope John XXIII was his desire to give the Church an aspect at once more maternal and more fraternal. For he well knew that, for the pagan world, this would be a witness of the fatherhood of God and an answer to the atheism of the masses.

This superficial survey is too rapid to display any subtlety, but it is enough to show that each Christian, and the Church herself, must delve deeply beneath the challenge of contagious unbelief and examine themselves concerning their spiritual vitality, their missionary zeal, and the personal or collective witness which they bear.

Finally, each one must question himself on his faith. The Plenary Assembly of the French Episcopate wrote on 27 April 1960:

'More than ever, we must all live on faith, a genuine, vital and integral faith. If the Christian mission is to come to anything, it must be inspired by faith. If it does have an impact, it will be by faith ... This demands daring revisions in our habits of thought and action.'

Faith, then, must be the starting-point of the conversion of each Christian, if it is to be the point of arrival of the evangelization of a pagan world.

The way has been clearly shown by St John: 'And this is the victory that overcomes the world, our faith. Who is it that overcomes the world but he who believes that Jesus is the Son of God?' (1 John v, 4-5).

15.

A Personal Knowledge of the True God

> *'And this is eternal life, that they know thee the only true God, and Jesus Christ whom thou hast sent.'*
>
> John xvii, 3.

1. *From the 'good Lord' to the living God.* Many Christians do not know the true God, the Father, revealed by Jesus Christ. In their minds he is reduced to a vague and distant godhead, without distinguishing features, who never emerges from a vaguely menacing silence. If they are asked to name this divinity, they call him by a name that has nothing biblical about it, the 'good Lord'.[1] If they are asked to explain how they imagine this godhead, they describe a composite image which is a cross between Jupiter and Father Christmas with his long beard. The way in which far too many Christians speak to God is a revelation of their mentality. Their manner of living is still more significant: their moral life, as revealed in the confessional, seems to be mere obedience, not to a person, but to a law without a personality behind it; to commandments without an author. For them, the spiritual life is nothing more than a moral system, and virtue or the virtues are the absolute values. When God is reduced to being no more than a law, he impinges with all his weight on man, and the latter has only one desire, to free himself from him. What intimate and familiar ties can he have with him?

2. But Jesus has clearly indicated the road to be followed; in his prayer to his Father he says: 'And this is eternal life, that they know thee the only true God, and Jesus Christ whom thou hast sent' (John xvii, 3). Jesus called himself 'the door' of access to the

---

1. Let us hope that preachers will one day cease to prolong the grotesque existence of this 'good Lord' so far removed from the God of revelation.

Trinity (John x, 9), and affirmed that no one could go to the Father except by him (John xiv, 6).

Therefore it is Christ, in all the richness of his divine and human nature, whom the Christian must first discover.

We must avoid simplifying the face of Christ by diminishing it. He is certainly man, but we must not see him only as the human friend, the 'comrade'. He is certainly God, but we must not portray him as if the incarnation of the Word had never been, or as if the resurrection had caused the humanity of Christ to evaporate. Christ is inseparably God and man. His divinity and his humanity are both vital. The human risen Christ sits permanently at the right hand of the Father, the first-fruits of our own resurrection.

The face of Christ that humanity looks to today is precisely the face that he habitually revealed to his apostles—that of a saviour.

' "The God of Jesus Christ" has only ever revealed himself since the time of Adam as the God who saves mankind. He has believed in man and is bent on delivering him from what diminishes, mutilates, or crushes him. He has made him his heir. In their different ways, all the atheistic philosophers . . . whether of the nineteenth or of the twentieth century, have said the same thing: "If man is to live, God must die!" This saying probably sums up the thought of the unbelieving workers: "If we must rid ourselves of God in order finally to be interested in man, then let God die; let him disappear."

'But *if we believe in God as a saviour, if it is of this God that first our actions and then our words bear witness, I think that the workers, when they discover him behind their lives, will not reject him.* For the God of Christianity, who after all took on our human life, saves mankind by starting out from his real conditions of life, his earthly situation.'[1]

1. *L'Athéisme, tentation du monde, réveil des chrétiens.* Contribution of Père André Depierré, p. 136.

Unfortunately, as we know only too well from experience with the dechristianization of the workers' world, the conditions of work, housing, and insecurity of employment are often such that a normal Christian life is impossible for those living in these conditions. Now, Christ came to save man from his servitude, from every form of servitude.

The Christian of today must show his fellow-men the true face of Christ the Saviour, and exert all his strength in creating conditions which will enable the living Christ to realize his mission of salvation in the world of today. Only when this is done will it be possible for people to understand that Christ also saves from sin, from our sin.

Moreover, we must recognize ourselves as sinners. St Paul emphatically says of himself: 'But I am carnal, sold under sin. I do not understand my own actions. For I do not do what I want, but I do the very thing I hate . . . For I do not do the good I want, but the evil I do not want is what I do . . . Wretched man that I am! Who will deliver me from this body of death?' (Rom. vii, 14-24).

It is radically impossible to know Jesus our Saviour if we are not convinced that we are slaves of sin crying out for our freedom. In order to discover the vital link between Christ and ourselves, we must realize our need for him like prisoners who wait for one who is to deliver them from their chains. If not, Christ will remain outside us; he will not enter into our lives.

This sin, to which St Paul realizes he is sold, is that selfishness in all its forms which is the mark of original sin in us. We are full of selfishness in every form, and express it by external actions, or more subtly, by a blindness that prevents our recognizing the face of Christ under the appearances which it takes. And the truth is that our sins of omission express our original selfishness more truly than our sinful actions do.

It is not easy for us to place ourselves in the ranks of sinners because our natural complacency inclines us to rank ourselves spontaneously with the just. Nevertheless, for want of this self-discovery, the Christian life of many of us grows faint. We must learn to know ourselves clearly, to know what is in 'the man that I am'. There are two sources of this experience—the contemplation of God's holiness which, as in the case of Isaiah (chap. vi) and Job (chap. xlii) induces an acute sense of our human wretchedness and an urgent need of God's mercy; and a penetrating and ruthless contemplation of ourselves.

Anyone who has an understanding of God, 'who tries the heart and the mind', knows well that he himself is not righteous and that his only hope is in God's mercy. The only obstacle, the only screen between Christ the Saviour and ourselves is pride that does not know its own wretchedness. But wretchedness itself does not constitute an obstacle. On the contrary, it appeals for and obtains mercy.

It is in this salvation brought to us by Christ that the divine sonship which he has communicated to us consists. Here it is the entire human being who is transformed and made divine, since body and soul are inseparably united. The Fathers of the Church and the liturgy itself—for instance, the prefaces for Christmas, the Epiphany, Easter, the Ascension and Pentecost—tirelessly remind us that the Word of God has taken a truly human nature, 'that he might grant unto us to be sharers in his own divinity'. And this is the basis, the dual basis, of the dignity of man, of every human person. We have been truly raised to God's level by the incarnation of the Son of God. This explains the attitude of the Christian who has not discovered this deep transformation effected, not only in himself, but in every man, and who consequently shows himself incapable of knowing Christ. But we shall return to this subject later.

3. It is in this way that *Christ leads us to the Father and reveals him to us*. He is the true way that leads to this discovery essential for the Christian. No one can know the Father unless Chist leads him to him. In effect, he who comes to know Christ, becomes

imbued with Christ's respect and love for his Father, and can no longer undervalue the person of the Father. The Father is certainly infinitely good and merciful, but he is also Almighty God.

By going to the Father with Christ we eliminate the risk of seeing only his goodness and not his demands. The goodness of Father does not lower him to our reach; it raises us towards him. 'The Father', as St Irenaeus says, 'is God invisible.' It is to him that those noble liturgical praises: '*Domine, Sancte Pater, omnipotens, aeterne Deus*', are addressed.

But the Father has 'first loved us' (1 John iv, 19); he 'so loved the world that he gave his only Son' (John iii, 16); 'the Father himself loves' us (John xvi, 27), as Jesus says. Hence, 'we know and believe the love God has for us' (1 John iv, 16). A Christian who has discovered the living God is one who believes in the Father's personal love for him and who makes this personal, positive and faithful love the corner-stone of his whole human, spiritual, and apostolic life. Until he is convinced of it, he is only a beginner. Once he begins to believe in it and to live it, he senses what spiritual maturity is. And the spirit of sonship, which is the essence of spiritual childhood, is also maturity of soul.[1]

The mature Christian prays to the Father. He has a sense of his honour and glory. The reign of God's kingdom in the world becomes his deepest wish. For him, the Mass is no longer a mere ceremony or even the occasion for adoring Christ, but the time when he unites himself to Christ in his adoration of the Father and in his permanent self-offering to him. Such love of the Father is

---

1. Christians sometimes experience a real psychological difficulty in considering God as a father. This can stem from a painful childhood experience of an unworthy or brutal father human. If they overcome this obstacle they discover the wonders of a true father's love and the possibility of reaching that maturity of soul of which we have been speaking. God has not taken the name 'Father' in order to rely on the experience of men. He is the one Father (Matt. xxiii, 9). To understand the divine paternity we must place ourselves, not on the psychological plane but on the plane of being. God is the one true Father, and it is from him that all fatherhood, in heaven and on earth, takes its name and its reality (Eph. iii, 15).

the unifying principle of a human and Christian life, because the filial love of God is the basis of love of our neighbour. And the psychological error of communism consists in wishing all men to be brothers without having a common Father.

In the parable of the prodigal son, which throws so much light not only on the mind of the heavenly Father, but also on the minds of his children, it is easy to see that the elder son has no true filial love since he does not love his own brother. Compared with his father, he has only the mentality of a mercenary creditor who demands his rights. In this attitude he scornfully calls his brother 'this son of yours . . .' (Luke xv, 30), whereas the erring son, whatever his failings, has the essential quality of filial love. He has squandered everything, but he has never doubted his father's love. And what else matters to the father? The fact remains that those who humble themselves before the paternal mercy of God will have no trouble in maintaining a loving humility in their relationships with their fellows.

4. *For the Christian, the Holy Spirit also becomes a living person.* But the discovery of him is more mysterious. The Christian does not address himself to the Holy Spirit at first, because he will naturally pray less to him than to the Father and the Son. But the Holy Spirit is the bond of love. Every time the Christian turns to his heavenly Father, it is the Holy Spirit who puts his name on his lips and his love in his heart. 'When we cry, "Abba! Father!" it is the Spirit himself bearing witness with our spirit that we are children of God' (Rom. viii, 15-16).

He animates our prayer and 'helps us in our weakness'. 'For we do not know how to pray as we ought, but the Spirit himself intercedes for us' (Rom. viii, 26).

Every time the Christian places himself in the presence of Christ and unites himself with him, it is the Holy Spirit who makes his prayer possible, because no one can even pronounce the name of Jesus or confess him as Lord 'except by the Holy Spirit' (1 Cor. xii, 3).

Every time the Christian makes his revision of life[1] and realizes that all those he passes in the street or meets at work are his brothers and that he is commanded to love them truly in the name of God, it is the Holy Spirit who opens his eyes to this fact, and wakens his fraternal love (Rom. v, 5). The Holy Spirit was present at each stage of the early Church's growth (cf. the Acts of the Apostles). Today too he is the Counsellor who calls and holds the Church together by ceaselessly wakening the hearts of Christians. He is the soul of the apostles of today, of the convinced and active laymen and women who are everywhere discovering their responsibility in the world and in the Church. There is no divine unrest or missionary action that is not awakened by the Holy Spirit.

It is the Holy Spirit who loves in us. The Christian who has discovered the living God cannot cease to grow in love, and each instance of that growth is the work of the Holy Spirit. The Christian discovers the Holy Spirit by being animated by him.

5. *The Christian who has discovered the living God, Father, Son and Holy Spirit, seeks his presence unceasingly in the countenances which the Lord assumes.* For God is here, Christ is among us, and we do not recognize him. We have sometimes been astonished at the Jews' lack of understanding in the time of Jesus. All of us would have been equally blind. What is more, we go on being blind, constantly, for Christ is with us and we do not see him.

John the Baptist said: 'Among you stands one whom you do not know' (John i, 26). These prophetic words are still true today, and knock at the doors of our hearts. And it is the same with so many other sayings: 'He came to his own, and his own received him not' (John i, 11); 'Have I been with you so long, and yet you do not know me' (John xiv, 9); 'I was hungry . . . I was naked . . . I was in prison' (Matt. xxv, 35-45); 'I am Jesus whom you are persecuting' (Acts ix, 5).

All these texts ring true today. Père Depierre writes:

1. A spiritual exercise practised in Catholic lay movements.

'In a town in France where some four thousand Algerians live, not one of the several hundreds of them whom we knew had not at least been ridiculed and insulted during the period of great tension in the autumn of 1961. Most of them had been maltreated—beaten up in the streets, in their homes, or at night in their lodgings. All of them had been humiliated. Many had simply disappeared, others had been arrested, then imprisoned, for no reason at all, on their way home from work. And all this maltreatment was their daily bread, as it were. Everyone could see these scenes of violence in his own street. One could hardly walk two steps to the grocer's or the *metro* without seeing Algerians being illtreated . . .

'Some of the priests in the town, and a few Christian workers and members of Catholic Action, felt we had to do something about it, or at least make some protest . . . Not one practising Catholic from the three largest parishes in the town had spoken to a priest about what was happening. So four thousand brothers of Jesus Christ, four thousand sons of God, the poorest, the most beloved of God, flesh of our flesh, our street neighbours, could be treated in a beastly manner without any reaction from a single Christian out of fifteen hundred or two thousand practising adults in the town (with the exception of one or two active members of the Christian Workers movement). That is the calamity. "The God of those people does not interest our comrades." He is too far from men, too much of a stranger to the fate of the poor.'[1]

This text is just as relevant to the present time and our own environment, and will continue to be so. The Algerian war is over, and did not affect us in this country as it affected France. But we have our own coloured populations, our own immigrants, who arrive and become submerged, nameless and unknown, in the working-class quarters of the towns. From now on

1. Contribution by Père Depierre on the difficulty of Christian life in a working class milieu, *op. cit.*, pp. 136-139.

there will be people of all colours and nationalities in every town clamouring to pick up the crumbs that fall from the tables of the rich—that is to say—from us. But what about the Catholics of our parishes! Few of them even know of these people's existence. Parishes that maintain a life they claim to be spiritual and yet remain absolutely indifferent to the fate of the poor have no right to call themselves Christian communities. They do not know; they do not see. These people are children of God and brothers of Jesus Christ. They represent Jesus Christ himself. To ignore them, is to ignore Christ.

But the Christian who has discovered the living God sees him in each one of his brothers, more especially in the poorest and the most despised: 'Can anything good come out of Nazareth?' (John i, 46). He is aware that he will never be able to meet God in personal prayer without first meeting him in his brothers.[1]

God is not indifferent to the fate of each separate person who is poor, but he accepts the terrible risk of not manifesting his love for them, his special love for the under-privileged, except through the mediation of Christians. Yet most Christians are sublimely unaware of the fate of those who are being crushed by their

1. Père Depierre continues:

'Recently we asked some priests about women in the town who work in industry. In the thirty or so radio-electric factories twenty thousand women work on conveyor belts for an average of fifty-five hours per week, at a speed which has certainly doubled in the last five to ten years. (In one factory where friends of mine work, the speed has doubled in a single year. In the factory opposite us—though this is illegal—women work on night-shifts.) We realized that the whole eternal being of these women was endangered—their physical life, their nerves, their emotional life, their home life, the rearing of their children, even the very possibility of their having children, and finally, their spiritual life. All their life, from fourteen to sixty-five, is occupied in these murderous factories, these cemeteries of the soul. This is certainly something that affects their eternal life. One of us said: "The Church should say or do something . . ." In fact, nothing happened, though a *curé* of one of the three parishes had heard about these conditions. "A woman parishioner of mine told me about it once", he said. I repeat that there are fifteen to twenty thousand women working in these conditions. How can you expect these women and their families to be interested in a God apparently so indifferent to their fate?' *Op. cit.*, p. 137.

working conditions. Today, in our highly developed and affluent Western European society, new forms of poverty are arising. In both town and country the conditions of work are destroying human life, domestic life, and the life of the soul. What is the attitude of 'good Catholics' to all this? If a priest in his parish or a bishop in his diocese draws their attention to these unnatural conditions, he finds himself faced with the hostility and insults of the Pharisees to Christ for interesting himself in tax-collectors and sinners.

But a Christian who has discovered the living God immediately feels his heart moved by all the suffering of his brothers, and the unjust conditions under which they live. And he knows that he will never be able to stand before his heavenly Father in prayer nor have communion with Christ, unless he has communion with his brothers in their undeserved misery.

Again Père Depierre says:

'It is said that the working classes have never been evangelized. That is only half the point. The political and economic systems, the social structures born of the industrial revolution in the nineteenth century, have never been evangelized. I would venture to say that *neither the institutions of this industrial society nor its morals and customs*—the question of the length of working hours, for instance—*have ever been regarded as relevant to the primary requirements of the Gospel*. If something of what our Lord demanded of the Jewish people regarding the distribution of land, or the treatment of servants and the sharing of goods with them, were applied in industry, the world would be very different from the world around us, the world on which we depend, and which takes from the workers all their human destiny and all their liberty from youth to death. *Our industrial world has never been evangelized. It has not been even touched by the Christian revelation. It is the very antithesis of the beatitudes.* In spite of occasional personal exceptions among employers, directors, technicians, and lay apostles, this world is not Christian. It is not even Jewish. The workers live in a pre-biblical, barbaric world.'[1]

6. The Christian who has discovered the living God also learns to *read the Gospel* in a new way, that is to say, to read it *in the framework of his daily life*. In this way he hears the voice of God speaking to him today, and he discovers a new form of intimacy with him.

Doubtless his conversion has enabled him to make great advances in the spirit of the Gospel, but for a long time he has been 'hearing' the Gospel at Mass on Sundays and feast days. He has remained detached from the Bible, which he has found fossilized after twenty centuries. In short, he does not feel it concerns him.

And then, one day before or after his conversion—it does not matter which—he begins actively to read the Bible and to find spiritual nourishment in it. This spiritual nourishment eventually begins to take on life. The Gospel becomes a message sent to him, bearing his name and address. From the signs, parables and images used by Christ for the people of his time, he learns to distinguish what is always valid and therefore relevant to the present. Better still, if he has the opportunity of being formed in the revision of life practised in Catholic Action movements, he will become capable of interpreting, or rather understanding the application of Christ's words to the present day. It is in this way that the Gospel of daily life becomes clear to him, and the voice of Christ familiar.

7. Finally, the Christian who has discovered the living God cannot fail one day to *discover the Church*. Of course, if he has found God, and has heard the voice of the Lord, it can only be through the mediation of the Church. But he does not know this at first, and it will take him a more or less lengthy time to

1. *Op. cit.,* p. 139.

discover it. Here again it is a matter of slow growth. This slowness is bound up with the fact pointed out earlier: that the Church is not always discernible in her visible signs.

A convert needs a community in which he can live his faith, for Christianity is of its very essence a matter of community and brotherliness. It is impossible for a man to discover himself to be a son of the heavenly Father without experiencing a compulsive need to meet brethren with whom he can pray and hold dialogue. What kind of community will receive him? We have seen only too often that the parish, especially in a town, is too extensive and too full of organized activities to provide the kind of atmosphere he needs.

It is necessary for him to find a milieu less vast and anonymous, some intermediate circle where he can find coreligionists who will help him to live as a son of God.

Normally this should be the lay apostolate team drawn from the milieu to which he belongs. But it often happens, for reasons we shall try to analyse in the following chapter, that he cannot find a climate that suits him in these teams. The new convert has a long way to go before he becomes acclimatized to the visible organizations of the Church that are at his disposal. This is why there must be other intermediate communities, friendly, unofficial groups, between the pagan world in which he has lived and the official parishes, the visible and patent signs of the Church. In these groups he will feel at ease during the necessary period of acclimatization. That is also why it is so good that priests and formed Christians should join these relay stations of the faith and bring to them an extreme openness of heart, great humility and inexhaustable patience to enable them to accept and listen to anyone who comes from a state of unbelief and discovers the living God. Their task is to reveal by their approachability, humility and patience the maternal Church that has already accepted the new convert without his knowing it.

Such a person's path of discovery of the Church will lie not only on the affective, but also on the intellectual plane. The reading of the Bible—under direction, of course—will be helpful to him here. Modern man, who finds himself in a world stirred by forces all tending towards unification, and who daily breathes the air of Marxist evolutionism, will find intellectual and spiritual light in the discovery that his new-found faith is not just a body of ideas but a history that traces the ascent of a people, the people of God. This story of the chosen people, of which the history of the Church is a continuation, will help the convert to understand the Church which is the Mystical Body of Christ and the mystery or our faith.

8. To conclude this chapter, we shall underline *some conditions of the growth of faith* which depend on the Christian himself. For if we have succeeded above in showing that this growth is the work of the Holy Spirit, it is no less true to say that a humble human collaboration is called for.

This collaboration consists primarily in prayer. The Christian who has discovered the living God cannot help praying, and putting all he has into his prayer. This is a sign of his conversion. Previously, he probably prayed and even prayed frequently, but felt impelled to do so by an obligation outside himself or by habit. But once he knows the living God, he cannot refrain from praying, praying constantly even. He is aware that he is living with Jesus Christ before the face of the Father and his prayer, even if wordless, is the necessary means of that dialogue which love demands.

This prayer, as we have said more than once, is nurtured on everything that human intercourse brings to it. It is impossible for anyone who has discovered his sonship of the heavenly Father not to open his eyes to his brothers, more especially to those whom Christ loves best. This is why a person living as a Christian is one who has a care for others, not only in his prayers but also in shouldering his responsibilities in the life of the world and of the Church.

CONCLUSION

We have outlined very imperfectly the path of one who has encountered the living God. He may have come from atheism or even from the ranks of the 'good Christians', but one day he discovered that God was a 'someone'—that he was the Father, that he was Jesus Christ, that he was the Holy Spirit. The paths of converts differ widely one from another, but all have certain points in common which we would underline:

(a) The discovery of God is always an elevation of the person. To know that God loves us, that he knows us by name, that he has a plan and, as we might say, ambitions for us, brings about an affective enrichment of the heart and of the whole life, for time and eternity. Even on the simple human plane, to know oneself to be loved causes a marvellous growth of the personality. How much stronger is the reason for this when one discovers that one is loved by God himself!

(b) Because it is an elevation of the person converted, the discovery of God is also an elevation affecting everyone. The convert knows that there is in fact one single love, and that he whom he has just discovered, to his enrichment, is given him for others. God does not have some children whom he loves and others whom he does not love. He loves them all and his preference, if he has one—and he has said so often enough in the Gospels—is for poor Lazarus, for the sinner Zacchaeus, for the crucified thief, for those who are hungry, cold, or prisoners. Hence, one who has truly discovered God spends his time and life loving those whom God loves best in order that his human love may become a revelation of God for them.

This is why he never comes to the end of the path on which the Holy Spirit has sent him. The education of his spiritual outlook continues and his faith grows unceasingly.

16

From Human Hope to Theological Hope

ONE who has a right understanding of God, and has discovered him as a living person, should be able to attain true theological hope. This hope has a wide range. It sees daily life as being entirely in the hands of the Father, even in its humblest details; it sees the spiritual life and its growth as being dependent above all on the grace of God; it sees the apostolic life as obedience to mysterious laws inaugurated by the death and resurrection of Christ, the source of all its fruitfulness. At the same time it sees in advance the happiness of heaven, which our Lord has promised us by calling us to rise with him.

1. The measure of divine hope in *daily life* is indicated by our Lord himself in words reported by St Matthew, words which the majority of Christians cannot hear without impatience and incomprehension: 'You cannot serve God and mammon' (money). This is the key-text. And Jesus continues:

'Therefore I tell you, do not be anxious about your life, what you shall eat or what you shall drink, nor about your body what you shall put on. Is not life more than food, and the body more than clothing? Look at the birds of the air: they neither sow nor reap nor gather into barns, and yet your heavenly Father feeds them. Are you not of more value than they? And which of you by being anxious can add one cubit to his span of life? And why are you anxious about clothing? Consider the lilies of the field, how they grow; they neither toil nor spin; yet I tell you, even Solomon in all his glory was not arrayed like one of these. But if God so clothes the grass of the field, which today is alive and tomorrow is thrown into the oven, will he not much more clothe you, O men of little faith?

Therefore do not be anxious, saying, "What shall we eat?" or "What shall we drink?" or "What shall we wear?" For the Gentiles seek all these things; and your heavenly Father knows that you need them all. But seek first his kingdom and his righteousness, and all these things shall be yours as well. Therefore do not be anxious about tomorrow, for tomorrow will be anxious for itself. Let the day's own trouble be sufficient for the day' (Matt. vi, 24-34).

Those who are irritated by this text declare that Christ is not realistic, or that he encourages laziness. He is not realistic because he ignores the laws of economics. He ignores the fact that today two-thirds of the human race are undernourished. They willingly reproach him, as they reproach the pope and the bishops when they take a stand on social problems, with being ignorant of political and social science and intervening in a sphere in which they are not competent. It is useless to point out to these Christians that widespread hunger is a 'privilege' of our age and a result of the present economic system, that the inhumanity, if not slavery, of the conditions of work is in certain respects much worse than the servitude in which so many human beings lived in ancient times. We must begin by profoundly accepting the fact that Christ is truth and life itself and that today he speaks to the heart of each Christian with the very force and relevance of God. Those who do not admit with wholehearted conviction that Christ is the Word of the living God, cannot understand his teachings, whatever explanations we strive to give them. It is also necessary to begin by assenting with all our being to the principles affirmed by Christ: 'No one can serve two masters; . . . You cannot serve God and mammon.' 'But seek first his kingdom and his righteousness, and all these things shall be yours as well' (Matt. vi, 24, 33).

God is not an alibi; he is not an extra guarantee added to a life organized on purely human lines; he is not an insurance against possible failure. Either he is everything to the Christians or, in spite of appearances, he is nothing at all. For it is very easy to plan our life and the lives of our family with perfect human wisdom as if God did not exist, and then to add a touch of piety here and there in the way of religious practices, and even sacraments. There is always a great risk of God remaining on the surface of lives into which he is not invited to enter.

All who live like this remain on the level of human hope and do not reach the plane of spiritual hope where God, who is master of the impossible, acts. How many parents and teachers direct and encourage their children's studies as if the horizon of life were limited to the face of this passing world! They keep a good conscience throughout by giving this human construction a slight veneer of Christianity, the conventional minimum of religious practice, at the right times inducing the children to pray for success in their examinations. Let it be clearly understood that we are not meant to refrain from being provident and working for success. Moreover, the Sermon on the Mount ends by reminding us of the obligation of daily work. But the main question is this: Is God really God for those who live in this way? What is his place in their lives? Does he take first place? In their legitimate provision for the future of their children, is God given first place? Is God everything to them? Or is human effort virtually everything, and God relegated to the position of an alibi?

Père Depierre writes:

'How could modern pagans come to believe in eternal life—not only in its promised extension after the resurrection of the body, but in the eternal life which I certainly reckon we are already launched on with our Lord—since the majority of Christians do not believe in it? . . . When God speaks in the Old Testament of the heritage which the just have left to their children, it is not riches or the consideration of the powerful ones of this world, but the spiritual heritage—trust in God, wisdom, faith and charity. I do not see how people can come to believe in eternal life if Christians do not show practical belief in it by the witness of their lives.

'Theoretical explanations of God can say nothing to those who have not seen God living in the witnesses whom he has chosen from among those around them.'[1]

The principle on which all Christian life must be based is that God is God, that he has a claim on our whole heart, and that he directs and governs all things. If God is not at the core of our lives, we can only stay on the plane of human hope.

The pagans, Jesus said, act as they do because they do not know that they have a Father in heaven. But when God is at the core of our life and of all our legitimate works, we ascend to the plane of divine hope. The practical attitudes counselled by Jesus stem from there. 'Do not be anxious', says Jesus. 'Your Father knows that you need them.' Besides, all the worries that you give yourselves, all your anxieties will be of no avail, because all the worries in the world cannot prolong your span of life by one cubit. Do not add the worries of tomorrow to the passing day. God gives you your measure of trials each day and the grace to bear them, but he does not give you grace to bear the trials of tomorrow at the same time as those of the passing day. You ask the Father to give you *today* your daily bread and your spiritual bread. But you do not ask this bread for a week ahead because God loves you too much to give you stale bread.

Before we can attain to spiritual hope we must have discovered the living God and staked everything on him. Nor do we attain to this hope at one stroke. Here too, growth continues all through life under the action of the Holy Spirit who uses circumstances and events to form the soul in hope. But first the soul must be swept clear of its human ideas, its instinctive preoccupations, its fear of God's methods. This is why it is faced with 'trials' in the

1. *Op. cit.,* p. 140.

widest sense of the word—events which will be the means of 'proving' that God is so much at the core of our life that we consent to stake our all in his word, and to surrender ourselves to it.

These 'trials' have very varied aspects. Here it is not a question of spiritual trials, of which we shall speak later on, but of the divine will to which Christians have to submit in their everyday life. Illness, an unexpected and unwanted addition to the family, housing problems, unjust treatment by someone over us, professional troubles or failures. Each of these trials obliges the Christian to choose between two planes—the plane of human hope where no distractions or worldly pleasures can prevent worry from gnawing at the heart, or the plane of spiritual hope, where the first place is left to the action of God, with which human effort co-operates diligently.

The Christian who wishes to grow in spiritual hope is in fact driven to choose God, that is to say, to give to his discovery of the living God all its dynamic importance. Is God really God and master of the impossible for him in the fabric of his daily life?

This journey in divine hope is the only way to true and permanent joy. It is also the best means of bearing Christian witness, for those who have achieved Christian hope oblige others to wonder what the source of their serenity is. And we shall never be able to pass on the joy of our religion to others by revealing God to them unless we live in Christian hope.

This means beginning life anew each morning under the eyes of God, without reservation or thought for the morrow. If we do make provision or think of the morrow, we are still on the plane of human hope. In other words, it is only through complete detachment that we can attain spiritual hope.

Such a radical choice, which is yet bound up with the discovery of the living God, necessarily leads the Christian to a closer solidarity with his brothers who do not share his hope because they do not share his faith. Nothing is more universal than suffering, and the worst suffering is fear of a future more dark and gloomy than the present. Anyone who looks around him is aware that the number of people who live without human or spiritual hope is immense. He meets them at his work, in his town, perhaps in his home.

The Christian who becomes aware of this universal suffering cannot shut his eyes to it. His role is not to preach spiritual hope in words—which would be out of place and perhaps arrogant— but rather to share the suffering of all because he knows what suffering is. At the same time, he feels obliged to cherish human hope in the name of all those who have no spiritual hope. He has discovered the living God by an unmerited grace, and now that his life has a meaning and that he knows he is guided by a Father's hand, he remains the humble witness to the spiritual hope of the world.

'Now faith is the assurance of things hoped for, the conviction of things not seen' (Heb. xi, 1). But we must avoid misunderstanding as well as the accusation that we are advocating a shelving or evasion of the problems of our lives and of the world. On the contrary, we must enter into these problems with all our energy as Christians, constantly searching for God's will which expresses itself in these daily events, and actively collaborating with it by our obedience to him. Here again, our lives must bear witness to our hope in God's fatherly care.

2. The *spiritual life*, like our daily material life, in all its most humble details, gives us constant opportunities to pass from human hope to spiritual hope. The growth of the spiritual life is a collaboration with God, but a collaboration of a particular nature. Many spiritual writers have tried to describe it, for instance by saying that God carries out both the desire and the action in us, or again, by saying that God anticipates, accompanies and perfects man's action. But in fact it is impossible adequately to describe this collaboration of God's grace and man's action; one can only experience it, and discern some gleam of light in it.

We have already begun to describe the road which the Christian travels. When he sets out at his conversion he experiences great spiritual desires. He aspires to holiness, rather like St Bernard who read the lives of the saints at the beginning of his religious life and wrote: '*Quod isti et istae, cur non ego?*'—'if they did it, what is there to stop me?'

In short, the spiritual life in his eyes was an ascent he could make by his own brute force. He had the human hope of achieving sanctity, but spiritual hope was not yet a part of him. To arrive at spiritual hope, he was gradually to lose all his human hope. He was to learn that the spiritual life is not an ascent but a descent into the depths of his sinfulness. He was to learn that holiness is a word that must be reserved for God alone, and that for him the only right word was wretchedness.

As long as he imagined he was capable of something on his own, he had still to free himself from human hope, but in the measure that he staked everything on the mercy of God, spiritual hope was born in him.

We have said that in order to discover Christ as our saviour, we have to experience our own misery. To recognise that we are sinners is only part of the truth, for if we are to attain to a state of perfect spiritual hope we must see ourselves as *sinners saved* by Christ. True awareness of our wretchedness, true humility, far from throwing us back upon ourselves, opens us to the mercy of God. And the ascent to spiritual hope is only granted us when we recognize our wretchedness and offer it up to Christ.

This is the path St Paul travelled, and what he says about it helps us: 'Who will deliver me from this body of death?', he asks; and he gives the answer: 'The grace of God through Jesus Christ our Lord' (Rom. vii, 24–25); 'So it depends not upon man's will or exertion, but upon God's mercy' (Rom. ix, 16); 'What have you that you did not receive? If then you received it, why do you boast as if it were not a gift?' (1 Cor. iv, 7); 'Our sufficiency is from God' (2 Cor. iii, 5); 'If I must boast, I will boast of the things

which show my weakness' (2 Cor. xi, 30); 'I besought the Lord . . .
but he said to me: "My grace is sufficient for you, for my power
is made perfect in weakness." I will all the more gladly boast of
my weaknesses, that the power of Christ may rest upon me . . .
For when I am weak, then I am strong' (2 Cor. xii, 8-10).

Salvation by Christ is being continually effected in us. Salvation is often preached about as if it were only connected with
the time that follows death: we 'save' our soul. But it is now that
our Lord is saving us; 'now is the time of salvation.'

This is the teaching God gave his chosen people in the Psalms.
If we want to discover the dimensions of hope we should nourish
our prayer with the Psalms. And the Church's liturgy teaches us
the same lesson; the prayers in the Ordinary of the Mass, for
instance, can all be summed up in two absolutely complementary
phrases: the wretchedness of man, the mercy of God.

Many prayers in the Sunday Masses express at once an acute
sense of sin, joy, total peace, and absolute confidence in the mercy
of God; another example is in the collect for the Mass of St Jane
Frances de Chantal: 'De nostra infirmitate conscii, in tua virtute
confidimus—we recognize our weakness and rely on your
strength.' We should read all these texts, not dispassionately but
earnestly applying them to ourselves, for in this way the Church
will lead us to supernatural hope.

3. Every kind of *apostolic life*, whether of priests, religious, or
actively committed lay persons, requires this detachment of
self which is an essential condition of the transition from human
to spiritual hope.

Many priests are greatly tempted to discouragement. If they
have been placing their confidence in Catholic Action, and
especially in the Catholic Workers' movement, they feel that
they are making no headway at all. The slow task of training
lay apostles tries their zeal, which is eager for visible results.
They are so conditioned to the traditional priestly role of 'teaching' the word of God and 'administering' the sacraments that they

have great difficulty in waiting in patient self-effacement for the slow maturing of God's word. In the same way, priests in charge of parishes suffer from the inconsistency between actual faith and the 'signs' of faith. When they administer the sacraments, the signs of faith, year after year to people who for the most part have no real faith, one can understand how they weary of it all and begin to doubt their ministry.[1]

But all, priests and lay apostles alike, need to reflect on their own apostolate in order to accept that stripping of all human hope which the Holy Spirit demands of them as the condition for arriving at spiritual hope. On this path they will probably pass through three stages.

In the first stage they discover their apostolate—the movement to which they belong or are chaplains, as the case may be—to be an entirely valid and quite realistic means. The danger is that they rely too much on this very human level. Their prayer and their spiritual life in general now run the risk of remaining outside and unconnected with their activities. And if they feel they are succeeding, they are liable to make their movement an end in itself and so form something esoteric. Yet if they founder, their discouragement injures the faith they have placed in their movement. This is why it is so necessary that they should reach a second stage in their growth.

They remain faithful to their method which may be a wholly legitimate one; but after experiencing defeat, they come to realize that since Christ died on Calvary, a share in the trial of the mystery of cross and passion and in the hope of the mystery of his resurrection, forms an essential part of every apostle's life. This second stage marks progress, since spiritual and apostolic life tend to become unified; prayer now nurtures the apostolate, and apostolic experience nurtures prayer.

But here there is another danger lying in wait for them, and we

1. See in J. Loew and G. M. Cottier, *Dynamisme de la foi et incroyance* (Paris, 1963), the original letter of M. Lochet, pp. 103-127.

must see it clearly. It is the danger of the good conscience of those who 'understand'. Their apostolic technique, corrected by faith, is well in focus, but their hearts are not open to others— to the free lances, those without position, those whose commitment is not 'valid', and who do not join *their* association, trade union, or team, as the case may be. With the best intentions in the world they form a Christian ghetto, and it is this mentality which kills all missionary spirit. As Karl Rahner says:

'For a certain type of deeply convinced, earnest militant Catholic, whose cultural level is rather primitive, the idea of entrenching himself in a ghetto is dangerously attractive; it is even religiously alluring. Indeed, it gives the impression of seeking only the kingdom of God. Here we are, all friends together, and we can behave as though there are only Christians in the world. The ghetto policy consists in thinking of the Church not only as the autonomous community of salvation (which she is) but as an autonomous society in every field . . . For example, every statesman who makes his Easter duty is a great statesman, any others are *a priori* suspect . . . This results in anti-clerical feeling, which is not always an effect of malice and hatred for God.'[1]

The ghetto danger threatens not only the traditional institutions of the Church but also the more recent ones—the specialized Catholic Action movements, for instance. It is only too easy to replace the clericalism of the clergy by a kind of clericalism of the laity which might be called 'laicism'.

Lay apostles must therefore clarify their outlook in the light of the Gospel. The Church asks them to take on a commitment, and she asks it insistently. The Christian must be neither a parasite of the world, profiting by advantages he has not helped to create, nor a parasite of the Church.

1. K. Rahner, *Mission and Grace,* (London, 1963), pp. 43-44.

'Each one has his part to play in the destiny of the country. Therefore each one has the right to interpret its interests, and the liberty and obligation to take on his social, civic and political responsibilities. To abstain from doing so is no trivial sin.'[1]

But temporal commitment must be kept in its right place. It is a second—not a secondary—vocation, which presupposes a first vocation to be members of a kingdom that is not of this world. The danger consists in the committed Christian throwing himself into temporal commitment as if it were an alibi that dispenses him from a life of faith; as if the one took the place of the other. Another and greater danger is that of cherishing a proud consciousness of belonging to a category of people who are highly thought of in the Church today. And this is why lay apostles must move on to a final stage.

At this stage they conserve all they have acquired in the preceding stages—faith in their movement, confidence in its methods, fidelity to their commitment. But their aim is higher. They live in Christ and share his suffering when they see him ignored and despised. They do not look down on anyone. On the contrary, they are at the service of their brothers, and look up to them. They do not limit the dynamism of their faith to one method, one structure, one institution. They participate in it without making it an end in itself, and they love and respect those who work in other fields.

4. Finally, there is one last dimension of the spiritual hope of the Christian. He awaits the *return of Christ;* for our Lord has promised that he will return. He looks forward to 'the city that has foundations, whose builder and maker is God' (Heb. xi, 10). He awaits 'a new heaven and a new earth' (Rev. xxi, 1). When this hope is preached to Catholics they are somewhat astonished— and in any case preachers seldom venture to speak of it. The fact

1. Declaration of the Assembly of Cardinals and Archbishops, 13 October, 1961.

is that neither clergy nor laity take it really seriously. Nevertheless it is one of the points on which the New Testament is most explicit. The expectation of the return of Christ was a particularly marked feature of the spirituality of the first century. 'Come, Lord Jesus'—*Maran atha!* The devout Jews whom we meet at the dawn of the New Testament—Simeon, Zechariah, and others— live 'awaiting the redemption of Israel'. Similarly, the Christians of today who have truly encountered the living God, know themselves to be awaiting the return of Christ.

Father Congar writes:

'Is it not remarkable that the Credo begins with the words "I believe", and ends with the words "*exspecto*", "I await"? The Christian life is equally and inseparably a matter of believing and awaiting. It is faith in Jesus Christ and waiting for Jesus Christ.

'A great number of our contemporaries are truly animated by a spiritual hope, a goal perhaps far ahead of us and towards which they are trying to impel the course of history. We, too, have our hope, but we know the end towards which the world is moving. All is directed towards Christ's final victory over death. With his resurrection a new order of things began. Easter Sunday is proceeding towards its consummation in the resurrection of all of us and the establishment of a complete and sovereign kingdom of God . . .

'Do we truly believe, as is said in Revelation, that he will wipe all the tears from our eyes one day? Ah, when it is a matter of a worldly victory or of a temporal deliverance, we know what desire and hope are.

'If it is a matter of the coming of a friend of flesh and blood, we know too what waiting for and desiring his coming is. Religious feelings are normally more discreet and serene, but they should be just as real, and occupy an effective place in our lives. Let us live in the expectation and desire of the return of our Lord; of his justice and his kingdom.'[1]

It must not be said that this is merely a way to escape from the difficulties of life and of man's despair. Spiritual hope is a gift of God, and the Christian who has discovered the living God must unite within his heart the values of this earth, the good things created by God, and the spiritual hope of things invisible. True, it is a difficult attitude to acquire, but Christ did not bring us an easy solution to the problems of life.

The author of the epistle to the Hebrews, writing to people tried by persecutions, insisted on this eschatological dimension of hope. And St Peter wrote to the first Christians words which still apply today: 'Blessed be the God and Father of our Lord Jesus Christ! By his great mercy we have been born anew to *a living hope* through the resurrection of Jesus Christ from the dead, and to an inheritance which is imperishable, undefiled, and unfading, kept in heaven for you . . . at the revelation of Jesus Christ . . . and rejoice with unutterable and exalted joy' (1 Peter i, 3-8).

Having our hearts rooted in this hope certainly should not turn us away from the good things and the struggles of this world by a kind of nostalgia for heaven, but rather should give us the very dynamism of God's grace, for we know what we are living for. This world will not pass away but will be transformed in eternal life which has already been begun through the changes wrought by our Christian charity as we collaborate daily in God's ceaseless creation of the world.

1. Congar, *Les Voies du Dieu vivant*.

Growth in Faithfulness

THE author of the epistle to the Hebrews writes to the persecuted Christians lines which may serve as an introduction to this chapter:

'But recall the former days when, after you were enlightened, you endured a hard struggle with sufferings, sometimes being publicly exposed to abuse and affliction, and sometimes being partners with those so treated. For *you shared the sufferings of prisoners,* and you joyfully accepted the plundering of your property, since you knew that you yourselves had a better possession and an abiding one. Therefore do not throw away your confidence, which has a great reward. *For you have need of endurance, so that you may do the will of God* and receive what is promised . . . But we are not of those who shrink back and are destroyed, *but of those who have faith and keep their souls'* (Heb. x, 32-36, 39).

Faithfulness is the essential element of the faith of a Christian who has discovered the living God. It is this Christians' response to God's own faithfulness. God is faithful; that is to say, the love with which he loves us is powerful, constant, and final. Unfortunately, we can fail again and again, but God does not weary of loving us.

'When Israel was a child, I loved him, and out of Egypt I called my son. The more I called them, the more they went from me; they kept sacrificing to the Baals, and burning incense to idols. Yet it was I who taught Ephraim to walk, I took them up in my arms; but they did not know that I healed them. I led them with cords of compassion, with the bands of love, and I became to them as one who eases the yoke on their jaws, and I bent down to them and fed them . . . How can I give you up, O Ephraim! How can I hand you over, O Israel! . . . My heart recoils within me, my compassion grows warm and tender. I will not execute my fierce anger, I will not again destroy Ephraim; for I am God and not man, the Holy One in your midst, and I will not come to destroy' (Hosea xi, 1-9).

God is faithful, but our own faithfulness is always in doubt because of our frailty. While we do grow out of our unfaithfulness into a greater fidelity, yet it is only in death that this fidelity will be fixed. Meanwhile our steps are guided by the Holy Spirit, just as were those of Abraham, Mary and the apostles.

The fidelity of God is identical with the love he bears us. It is the same with us; all our progress in fidelity is a progress in love—love of God and love of our neighbour. In reality there is but one love, one single and unique theological virtue of charity which is born of the Holy Spirit, and passes into us and through us to our neighbour. Hence, the more we are born of the love of God, the more we love our neighbour. And the conscious communion of love, in which God takes the initiative in us, grows together with our conscious love for our neighbour.

I. YOU SHALL LOVE THE LORD

The first and great commandment—'You shall love the Lord your God with all your heart, and with all your soul, and with all your mind'—is stressed throughout the Bible. It is not a question of sentiment but of 'heart' in the biblical sense: that profound core of our being which is capable of choosing and persisting in its attachment until death. This commandment of absolute love is not reserved merely to some; it is given to all Christians by virtue of their baptism. This sacrament gives them, through the action of the Holy Spirit, the very love which is in

God. 'God's love has been poured into our hearts through the Holy Spirit which has been given to us' (Rom. v, 5). The Church does not consist of a select minority of priests and religious chosen to love God, and a mass of good people incapable of receiving such an honour. It is, of course, well known that a relatively recent tradition has reserved for the various forms of the religious life the misleading title of 'states of perfection'[1] *(status perfectionis acquiredae)*, but no intelligent person takes this form of words seriously at face value. We also realize that traditional Catholic teaching places the state of virginity above the married state. Here, however, we are not classifying abstract categories but addressing ourselves to real people. Every baptized person is called to the perfection of love by virtue of his baptism. When a Christian grows up and discovers the living God, his heart tells him clearly that he must love the Lord with all his strength. If he is married and has children, he still knows that his love of God comes first and only serves to deepen all human love. And a Christian who learns to love God with all his strength finds that, however imperfect his love is, he now loves his fellow-beings far more than before.

The perfection of love and the evangelical counsels are not meant merely for a few. They are for all, although the mode of realizing them varies with the different states of life.

This faithfulness and love of God should normally grow all through life under the action of the Holy Spirit. The process of this growth is the same as in the case of the apostles. Growth in faithfulness is not a gently progressive illumination, for nothing is less 'calm' than a Christian's growth in faith; it is marked by crises, difficulties, temptations, even failures. When a trial is surmounted, our faith in Christ acquires new light and our

1. St Thomas Aquinas says quite explicitly: 'The religious state of seeking perfection' *(Status perfectionis acquirendae)*, this perfection being one of charity communicated by God. And St Thomas was the first to recognize that being in a *state* of life does not amount to being perfect, though the state may in itself be one of perfection.

faithfulness takes on new strength. It is impossible to know Christ truly without entering more and more into the mystery of his death and resurrection and being 'born anew' at great cost. And our faithfulness does not grow unless our heavenly Father periodically prunes the branches of the vine that we are, making us suffer and bleed.

This is how we should interpret the trials with which our life is normally strewn, and which are the means we have seen God using in training the faith of Abraham, Mary and the apostles: the test of time, desolation of soul, impossible situations, contradictions, and even the shedding of blood.

For the Christian of today these trials are familiar enough. They are found in monotonous, harrassing, even inhuman work, insecurity of employment, illness in ourselves or in those dear to us, friction with someone close to us—a frequent cause of acute grief of heart; or again, real hindrance from those who should be helpful to us, or unexpected bereavement. Through all these experiences, sometimes hoping against hope, we must hold faithfully to God alone and to his love. And we need not be ashamed if we experience the temptation to give up.

We need not look for exceptional opportunities to practise renunciation; such occasions are rare. It is enough simply to recognize, accept and offer up the opportunities that daily life gives us of saying 'yes' to God. We must learn to interpret the meaning of our life and its trials. Naturally, the first shock knocks us over, but we must look at once for the message that God is thereby sending us. For all suffering has a twofold significance— a human meaning, which anyone can discover at a glance, and a divine meaning, in other words what God's intention is in sending a certain trial. In this way, we discover that we are sharing in the mystery of the death and resurrection of Christ, and that we are daily working together with him in the redemption of the world.

Every stage in our life, every crisis, great or small, is ordered to develop our faithfulness. Our faith steadily grows throughout our life in the measure that we participate in the mystery of Christ. The Christian who has discovered the living God must hold in his fingers the guiding thread that enables him to understand the meaning of his life. In the evening of his days he may not be able to say much more about Christ than in the first days of his conversion, but he will be able to speak of him in a different way, because he will have experienced more and more that Christ has been his very life.

The same laws of growth in faithfulness may be seen in the life of prayer. At the beginning of his spiritual road the convert discovers the consolation, the ease and even the delights of prayer, and he returns to it joyfully because it brings him sensible help.

If he then asks himself what makes him turn to God, he will see that it is first of all love of God, and he will be right in this. But if he examines his conscience more deeply he will recognize that he goes to God for the joy he finds in doing so, in short, out of self-love. Every step towards God is inextricably mingled with a self-seeking which we cannot eradicate by ourselves. Our own basic selfishness forms a screen in the depths of our being. This is why those words of the Old Testament: 'We shall surely die, for we have seen God' (Judges xiii, 22; Is. vi, 2 ff.; Ex. xxxiii, 18-22), are so applicable to the spiritual life.

Now, it is not in our power to take the initiative in regard to this death of self. But God himself intervenes in our life of prayer by depriving us of the sensible joy of his presence. He deprives us in some way of the faculty for prayer and effects in the eyes of our soul that ascent which leaves the soul living on naked faith. It is then that we learn the true meaning of faithfulness to God by being ready humbly to search for his presence in the dark; to hold firm, to bear the temptations and trials of our helplessness, and the succession of frustrations, in order to march towards him without seeing or perceiving him. It is by dint of holding firm and remaining faithful to prayer in times of dryness that we experience the realization of the last beatitude that Christ proclaimed before ascending to his Father: 'Blessed are those who have not seen and yet have believed' (John xx, 29).[1]

The growth of our faithfulness in prayer depends on how we face up to the difficulty—that humble form of the cross in our daily lives—which we experience at times when we find it almost impossible to pray. At such times faithfulness in searching resolutely in the darkness for the face of God is both the means and the proof of our love for him.

This is but one stage in the journey of each person, and with him, of all humanity, towards faith. There is a long struggle before victory comes. It is a long struggle for everyone, and the Christian who has discovered God knows himself to be jointly answerable for all those who do not yet see their way. And this is why he must believe that the darkness in which he struggles is the cross which he willingly bears for his fellow men in their journey towards the light. It is to this collaboration that God calls the convert, and this is precisely why he pays so very dearly for the discovery of the living God which his fellow men are one day to make.

St Thérèse of the Child Jesus wished to share in this way the bitter bread of all those who were far from God. And God took her at her word. She wrote:

> 'Is there any soul less tried than mine, to judge by appearances? Ah, if the trial I have been suffering for the past year could be seen, what surprise there would be! I sing what *I want to believe*. (She herself wrote this in capitals.) Being without the joys of faith, I try to do the works of faith.'

1. These words only apply indirectly to periods of darkness in faith and dryness in prayer, but they apply directly to the confidence we must have in the witness of the Church. Since, according to John xx, 21-23, Jesus had sent the Church its mission and given it the Holy Spirit, his words to Thomas have an application which means in practical terms: 'Blessed are those who believe in the simple witness of the Church.'

Other saints have suffered similar trials. At a certain stage of his life St Vincent de Paul could no longer say the words of the act of faith, so he wrote them down on a piece of paper which he always carried about with him. When the trial of faith was too severe, he put his hand on his chest to affirm by this gesture that he wished to believe what was beyond his capacity to believe. Such sacrificial offerings are necessary to win for others the grace of discovering the living God.

It is up this steep path that the Holy Spirit guides the Christian whose faithfulness he wishes to strengthen. And when one single person perseveres, the whole Church advances in faith with him.

II. THE LOVE OF OUR NEIGHBOUR

We never know whether we truly love God or not, whereas love of our neighbour is firm ground on which we cannot deceive ourselves.

St John writes:

'*We know that we have passed out of death into life, because we love the brethren.* He who does not love remains in death . . . By this we know love, that he laid down his life for us; and we ought to lay down our lives for the brethren. But if any one has the world's goods and sees his brother in need, yet closes his heart against him, how does God's love abide in him? Little children, let us not love in word or speech but *in deed and in truth*' (1 John iii, 14–18).

'Beloved, let us love one another; for love is of God, *and he who loves is born of God and knows God.* He who does not love does not know God; for *God is love.* In this the love of God was made manifest among us, that God sent his only Son into the world, so that we might live through him. In this is love, not that we loved God but that he loved us and sent his Son to be the expiation for our sins. Beloved, if God so loved us, we also ought to love one another. *No man has ever seen God; if we love one another, God abides in us* and his love is perfected in us . . . So we know and believe the love God has for us. *God is love, and he who abides in love abides in God, and God abides in him* . . . We love, because he first loved us. *If anyone says, "I love God," and hates his brother, he is a liar; for he who does not love his brother whom he has seen, cannot love God whom he has not seen.* And this commandment we have from him, that he who loves God should love his brother also' (1 John iv, 7-21).

We have not hesitated to quote St John at length, for this outstanding text shows clearly that love of others is intimately linked with love of God, and is its visible and authentic sign. But if this love of our neighbour is to be the means of our growth in fidelity to God, it must have certain dimensions.

1. In the first place, it must be *an imitation of Christ in his redemptive incarnation;* an imitation of him who, though he was God, as St Paul says, 'emptied himself, taking the form of a servant, being born in the likeness of men' (Phil. ii, 7).

This is why there are Christians today, including priests, who have resolved to share the lot of the workers in order to lead them one day to the heavenly Father. Their step is motivated in the first place by the desire to do what Christ would do if he were to come among us again. And this is precisely what he *did* do; he made himself one of those whom he came to save; he shared their work, their homes, their conditions, their insecurity, their sufferings. For it is useless to hope to bring salvation from above to those below; it is useless to preach without living with those who are to listen; it is useless to remain on the river-bank exhorting those who are in the water to swim courageously. Christ acted otherwise: 'And the Word became flesh and dwelt among us.'

Of course, those who resolve to follow Christ in this way in his redemptive incarnation take risks, as Christ himself did when he accepted all the humble realities of the human condition, all the opposition of family, friends and the conventional people of his time. He even sacrificed his life in this work. The priests who share certain conditions of working-class life today have accepted the consequences of this choice. They do this with the consent of the Church, but they also know that their Christian obedience has a redemptive value, for it means more for God and his glory than all the other finest techniques of the apostolate. They hope that one day they may have complete freedom to share the conditions of life of the workers to the full with a view to evangelizing them. Come what may, these priests and religious men and women, who make themselves the equals of men whom they wish to evangelize, will always meet with much opposition. When they are misunderstood by their own people they realise that they are suffering for the Church, for faithfulness to God and his Church always brings tensions to those who consecrate themselves to such work. But these very tensions are redemptive. Those who follow Christ in his incarnation in this way deserve to be called true missionaries, for with them the witness of shared life prepares for and supports the ministry of the word.

2. A second dimension of faithfulness as shown in the love of our neighbour is *the preference given to the poorest* in a service which should exclude nobody. Never before has so much been written about poverty in the Church, and this shows how much the Holy Spirit has been at work. But since we are addressing ourselves to Christians who have discovered the living God, we would urge them to see his countenance in the poorest, in those most deprived of the good things of life—of culture, health, liberty, human affection. We venture to hope that their persevering action may put an end to the scandalous fact that the poor are barely tolerated today in many of our Christian assemblies.

3. A third dimension of brotherly charity is *universality*. We said earlier that it is necessary for the Church to be presented to the people of today through the outward sign of parish communi-

ties adapted to their outlook, on the human level. But at the same time, the life of the Christian who has discovered the living God must be adapted to the scale of the whole world. The Church is not limited to one apostolic group, or one parish, or even one diocese. The Church must be present wherever there are people, if she is to be the evangelical conscience of the world. And every serious Christian must extend his heart and his prayer to this universal dimension.

4. The Christian who has discovered God is also *passionately concerned for unity with his brothers*. Everywhere he encounters the mark of the devil, who is the author of discord and the father of lies. There is disunity between the apostles of the same movement and the people of the same parish or the same social layer. And most painful and striking of all is the division between people baptized in the same Christ.

The Christian who has discovered the living God bears within himself the principle of the unity he must spread in all humility and perseverence. And since it is a matter of bringing Christ to a world that does not know him, he is keenly aware that the unity of all Christians is an absolute condition of witness, and that there is no other. Just before consummating his sacrifice, Jesus prayed in anguish to his heavenly Father:

'I do not pray for these only, but also for those who believe in me . . . that they may all be one . . . so that the world may believe that thou hast sent me . . . that they may become perfectly one, so that the world may know that thou hast sent me and hast loved them' (John xvii, 20-23).

All these dimensions of brotherly charity oblige the Christian who has discovered the living God to open his heart to the full. He sees that on these steep paths he still has everything to learn, and that he must continually sacrifice his comfort, his apparently most legitimate needs, the respect of all those who know him, and even his 'good conscience'. But all this stripping of self is vital if the serious Christian is to grow in faithfulness; and he discovers little by little that each step he takes to meet his brother enables him to see the face of God more clearly. For there is only one love.

Conclusion

WE know now to what the call of God commits the Christian, and the response of faith that it demands of him.

1. It is a call as personal and yet universal as the call he addressed long ago to the father of all believers. The frontiers of Christianity have burst open and everyone now receives a mission as large as the world, the mission of the Church itself.

Abraham too received a universal task: 'And by you', Yahweh told him, 'all the families of the earth shall bless themselves' (Gen. xii, 3). And this promise was to be renewed repeatedly in the same terms (Gen. xviii, 18; xxii, 18; xxvi, 4; xxviii, 14; Acts iii, 25; Gal. iii, 8). Mary likewise realized that the call she had heard was for all: 'For behold, henceforth all generations will call me blessed' (Luke i, 48). Similarly the Apostles only received the light so that they might spread it throughout the world: 'Go therefore and make disciples of all nations, baptizing them in the name of the Father and of the Son and of the Holy Spirit' (Matt. xxviii, 19); 'Go into all the world and preach the gospel to the whole creation' (Mark xvi, 15).

Today the Christian who has discovered the living God feels himself commissioned by him to communicate to others, in fact to everyone, all that he has 'seen'.

The world is saved. It has been saved by Christ's death and resurrection. The certainty of this is the corner-stone on which the Church has based her mission among those to whom she has been announcing the good news of this salvation for the last two thousand years. And yet each individual person must accept it himself and respond to it with faith.

It is above all in a man's heart that the decision is freely made whether or not to accept salvation from God. Further, each Christian who has made the response of faith to God's call is charged with spreading the good news to all his contemporaries. No doubt the faith is still transmitted from generation to generation, but it is also true to say that each generation is responsible for its own evangelization. And although God's call is always the same, its diffusion takes a form adapted to each time and place.

2. This is why the Christian who has found the living God should pay attention to this world and its cries and sufferings, and listen to the appeals that rise on all sides. The most insistent cries rise from those who hunger and thirst for justice and liberty. People no longer want to be colonized, nor even helped if this involves what they call neo-colonialism. The manual workers and the white-collar workers do not want their work continually threatened by the operation of economic laws which disregard the human being, and they are unwilling to have their insecurity relieved by benevolent measures that appear patronising. The poor make their voices heard in unison on a world scale. Here it is not a question of the kind of poor who in former ages were fed at monastery doors or had a place at the table of some Christian family on great feast-days. The poor nowadays are everywhere in the world. They are even among us here and now, when economic development brings well-being to an increasing number of workers, but when the demands of technical progress form new fringes of a sub-proletariat more wretched than before. These sub-proletariats are to be found more especially in that third of the world comprising 'the under-developed countries', where whole populations feel a gnawing hunger.

The Church must listen to their voices and bring them the answer that Christ has given us. This answer is the Church itself, not as the temporal power confronting others, nor as something weighed down with prosperous institutions, but the Church at the service of men and in their midst, the living voice of the Gospel and the conscience of mankind. It is this image of the Church that Pope John XXIII projected, and this is why even the least of his words and deeds have had such a repercussion. Each word he spoke answered man's subconscious hope, and a new dimension of the Gospel was revealed. A living Christian *is* the Church in whatever environment he is placed, but before he utters a single word he must allow the cry for justice and happiness which rises on all sides to find an echo in his heart.

It has been too long forgotten that God desires all men to be saved (1 Tim. ii, 4), body and soul; too long taken for granted that a privileged group of well-fed people should exist side by side with multitudes of people dying of hunger. And how quickly it has been assumed that Christians come largely from the well-fed! Nowadays real Christians can no longer tolerate this, and the Church has an opportunity to preach the Gospel to the poor, who are only now beginning to catch a glimpse of their place in the Church.

It is only when all this has happened that the Church will be able to proclaim the full dimensions of its hope. Certainly this hope transcends all human hopes, even the most legitimate ones, but it can only be preached when man's heart receives a human answer to human needs.

3. The Christian who has discovered the living God has a challenging task before him. It is true enough that modern atheism is militant and Marxism attractive, but never before has the world experienced such a thirst for the 'unknown God' as today. This is why the Christian who listens to his fellow-men can speak to them in their own language about the God he knows personally, and about the hope and faithfulness God demands. He discovers by degrees that the light he received when first converted increases little by little in the course of his life, in spite of his failures, or rather, because of them.

Faith grows because the Holy Spirit is always at work in all men of good will. It will never cease to grow, for the love of God is infinite, and the world is still far from being evangelized.

Also by Mgr Gerard Huyghe

TENSIONS
AND
CHANGE

The Problems of Religious Orders Today

The present day has brought new situations, new cultural environments, new human horizons, in which the witness of religious life must be expressed. The hundreds of congregations of religious men and women, who live and work according to their rule and special traditions are gradually coming to realise, not without tensions, that in order to bear witness in this modern world, they themselves must change.

As Cardinal Liénart says in his preface: 'The time has come for all religious families to make an examination of conscience. Why does not our congregation exercise the same effective influence as in former days? Why have we not been sufficiently alert in adapting ourselves to our times? Could we not respond more fully to the tremendous needs which can be satisfied only by renouncing certain customs, certain habits, which have no real ascetical or apostolic value?

'This book is an answer to these questions and this anxiety.'

Written with compassion and understanding of the life of the religious today, this book by Mgr Huyghe is a most valuable contribution to the present self-examination of religious orders.

Mgr G Huyghe and others

RELIGIOUS ORDERS IN THE MODERN WORLD

The theologians, bishops and monks who have contributed to this book give us, each from his own particular standpoint, a fuller understanding of the problems of religious life in a changing world.

The first section is concerned with providing clearer definitions of what religious life is about; the second deals with the place of religious in the wider context of the Church; the third suggests ways in which religious orders could profitably be reformed without losing sight of the ideals which inspired their founders.

The communal nature of religious life has made it necessary to have rules and constitutions and a definite status in Church law, all of which have led, like any written laws, to rigidity and to concentration on comparatively unimportant elements. Religious themselves have often been deeply concerned about the relevance to our own times of regulations devised for completely different social conditions, which have since lost most of their spiritual meaning and relevance.

The need for reappraisal and adaptation in the religious life is urgent. The impetus given by the Council to renewal in every section of the life of the Church is felt in the challenging and often controversial ideas in these essays.

Contributors: Mgr Joseph Urtasun, Mgr Charue, Mgr Gerard Huyghe, Karl Rahner, S.J., Jerome Hamer, O.P., Bernard Besret, S.O.Cist.